W9-BZR-787

JEWISH ITINERARIES
series edited by Annie Sacerdoti

In the same series

Lazio
Jewish
Itineraries
Places, history and art

by Bice Migliau *and* Micaela Procaccia

with Silvia Rebuzzi *and* Micaela Vitale

Marsilio
Regione Lazio

Our thanks to the Centre of Jewish Culture, the Historical Archives of the Jewish Community of Rome, Dora Liscia Bemporad, Anna Blayer Corcos, Laura Supino, Massimo Di Gioacchino, Anna Esposito, the UCEI Bibliographic Centre (especially Serena Terracina).

Bice Migliau wrote the introduction and texts for Rome.

Micaela Vitale wrote the texts for Porta Capena, the Forum and the Capitol (Rome, Itinerary V), the Vatican Museums and the Roman National Museum (Rome, Itinerary VIII), the Villa Torlonia and Vigna Randanini catacombs, the Appian Way (Rome, Itinerary IX) and Ancient Ostia.

Micaela Procaccia wrote the introduction and texts for Lazio.

Silvia Rebuzzi wrote the texts for the following localities: Acquapendente, Anticoli Corrado, Ariccia, Bagnoregio, Cantalupo Sabino, Cassino, Castelnuovo di Porto, Civitavecchia, Formello, Frascati, Frosinone, Gaeta, Genazzano, Genzano, Lanuvio, Montefiascone, Monte San Giovanni Campano, Nettuno, Orte, Palestrina, Priverno, Rignano Flaminio, Ronciglione, Sacrofano, Segni, Sezze, Sonnino, Soriano nel Cimino, Subiaco, Terracina, Tivoli, Velletri, Vitorchiano.

Annie Sacerdoti wrote the introductory texts to the individual towns and cities.

Photography by
Valerio Ricciardi
Design
Tapiro, Venice
Translated from the Italian by
Gus Barker
English editing by
Langstint, Isola del Piano (PS)
Typesetting
Chanan Zass, Mestre
Editing
Annalisa Longega

Cover picture: Detail of the embroidery work on an 18th-century *meil*, Rome, Museo ebraico

© 1997 by Marsilio® s.p.a. in Venice
ISBN 88-317-6819-0

Printed in November 1997 by La Grafica & Stampa Srl, Vicenza

Contents

LAZIO
JEWISH ITINERARIES

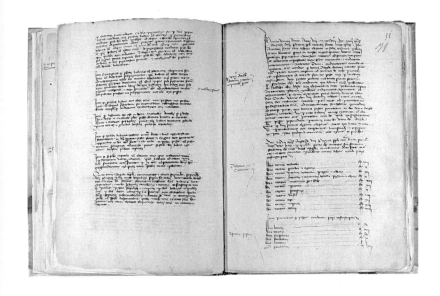

Chapters concerning the licence granted to the Jews of Rieti, dated 20 August 1408 (Archivio di Stato di Rieti, Archivio Comunale di Rieti, Riformanze 20, ff. 49 v-50 r.)

Introduction

In the late 13th century groups of Jews began rather suddenly to appear in the regions of central and northern Italy. Most had come from Rome in migratory waves that lasted up to the end of the century. Invited by the communal administrations in central and northern Italy, the Roman Jews, either individually or in groups, travelled the great consular highways to exercise the moneylending profession in new settlements. By the end of the 14th century, there were Jews of Roman origin throughout Lazio, Umbria, the Marches, and Tuscany. In these regions they formed relatively large communities in areas, where there had only ever previously been a temporary or occasional presence.

There are several explanations for this phenomenon. The rapid spread of Jewish banks in rural or semi-rural areas as well as in the towns is considered to be one of the main features of Italian Judaism from the 14th to 15th centuries, and the causes must be sought not only in economic factors but more importantly in social factors. The spread of Jewish settlements also provided expelled Jews with the opportunity to settle, thus allowing for a rise in population beyond the objective limits in the established places of residence. Another factor which must not be underestimated is that the presence of Jewish groups in several centres offered a kind of safety net against possible expulsion measures in any given town.

Whatever the reasons, the various provinces in Lazio are full of interesting evidence of the history of these migratory movements (also providing some support for more speculative theories). The papal administrative areas of the Patrimony of St Peter in Tuscia, Sabina, Campagna, Marittima and the area of the Castelli Romani (roughly corresponding to the present-day provinces of Viterbo, Rieti, Frosinone, Latina and Rome) provided the easiest natural settlement sites for the new Jewish communities, which sprang up at the end of the 13th century.

After the papal court had moved to Avignon, the city of Rome fell into one of its worst periods of economic and demographic decline.

This accentuated the Roman Jews' tendency to emigrate to new settlements.

Throughout the Middle Ages and Renaissance, the Patrimony of Saint Peter in Tuscia was the wealthiest and most important papal province in Lazio. The fertile Tiber Valley had a rich agricultural production, while the ports on the coastal belt (Corneto, Montalto and Civitavecchia) provided an excellent outlet for the cereal production.

There was also an efficient communications network: the rivers, especially the Tiber, but also smaller waterways such as the Fiora, Marta and Mignone, as well as the transverse roads and the Via Cassia. This good road and river network meant that transport was easy, and the first Jewish groups soon appeared in Viterbo, Orte, Corneto (now Tarquinia), Toscanella (now Tuscania), Acquapendente, and Montefiascone.

In 1326 we find the earliest collective mention of the Jews in the Patrimony in a register of the *Collettorie*, that is, concerning tax payments. The entry in the register records a sanction (a collective fine) meted out on all Jews in the area for failing to wear the badge. There were several generations of moneylending families in these towns, a sure sign of a local economy with a fairly high demand for cash.

In the second half of the 14th century, when Cardinal Egidio Albornoz brought the communes and signories back under papal control, he also took measures to administer the grain market (the Patrimony being one of the main papal producers and traders). This operation led to an urgent demand for money in Tuscia, and Jews soon arrived from Rome, while notarial sources record the spread of Jews in new localities in the province, adding to those who had arrived a few decades earlier.

In 1470 we find – again thanks to the *Collettorie* registers – Jews in Viterbo, Corneto, Acquapendente, Bagnoregio, Castro, Montefiascone, Orte, Tuscania, Vetralla, Anguillara and Cerveteri, making a total of fifty individuals. This figure is deceiving. In fact an individual taxpayer often paid for entourages of several whole households. The picture that emerges then is of fairly large settlements from the numerical point of view, distributed in various localities and mainly made up of the family of a loan-bank owner, who may have been accompanied by poorer families exercising various jobs, often associated with trading or small-time farming.

It was a similar story in the Sabina area, also easily accessible thanks to roads in all directions linking up the Rieti basin with the navigable network of the Tiber and the Via Salaria. And here, too, the presence of the Jews was recorded quite early, although initially it was rather provisional. There were only stable Jewish settlements around the end of the 14th century, as demonstrated by the *Costitutiones episcopatus sabiniensis* (Constitutions of the Sabina Diocese). Dating from 1342, these measures were based on earlier laws established by

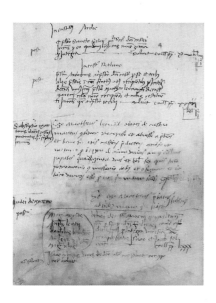

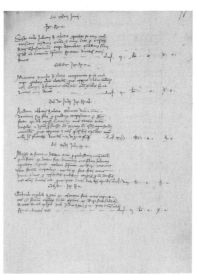

According to this document, a group of Jews in Marino paid taxes of 80 carlini papali *(8 ducats); but a wealthy Jew called Isahac refused to pay or even come to an agreement (Archivio di Stato, Camerale I, Collettorie, b. 1186, Patrimonio, reg. 3, f. 79 v.)*

In Ferentino on 26 July 1473 Mose di Masetto paid a fine of 8 ducats for having given his daughter Brunetta to be breast-fed by a Christian called Agnese *(Archivio di Stato di Roma, Camerale 1, Tesoreria di Campagna e Marittima, b. 2, reg. 5, f. 31 r.)*

Cori

the fourth Lateran Council of 1215. The Jews had to wear a white-coloured piece of clothing on top of their normal dress, so that Christians could recognise them. They could not appear in public on the days before Easter or openly eat meat during Lent. They were not allowed to work on Sundays nor on Christian feast days, nor have Christian wet nurses or servants. Similarly, Christians could not take part in Jewish banquets nor invite them to eat unleavened bread. They could not wash in the bathroom of a Jew, seek the services of Jewish physicians or take medicines prescribed by them, share a house with Jews, or appoint Jews to public office. Forced conversions were, however, prohibited.

There is no further mention of Jews in Sabina in the 14th century. This is probably due not only to a lack of documentary sources for the period but also to the provisional and precarious presence at a time when the province, with no large towns and a mainly rural economy was overwhelmed by the struggles between Roman noble families, especially the Orsini and the Savelli.

Cardinal Albornoz, papal legate and Bishop of Sabina, eventually brought some peace to at least some parts of the province and strengthened its strategic importance. In time the economy also improved with the growing production of cereals and oils, which were exported to the Roman market. This led to the need for greater credit, the premise for a stable settlement of Jews in the region. From the Aspra statutes of 1397 new, explicit and continuous references to the presence of Jewish moneylenders in the area began to be made. The references continued throughout the 15th century. In this case, too, the Jews had come from Rome. They had spread not only to Rieti but also to the villages and minor localities in the province, also finding suitable settlement sites in the Sabina area as an alternative to Rome which had grown increasingly impoverished since the time of the pope's Avignon exile.

In 1472, thanks to the usual recordings of taxes paid, we know there were Jews living in Magliano, Torano, Aspra, Montopoli, Nerola, Palombara, Monterotondo, Turri and Fara, as well as in Rieti. They mostly lived in very scattered small settlements (in practice almost only the family running a loan-bank). The Sabina Jews kept up their frequent contacts with Rome, and although moneylending was the main officially recognised activity justifying their presence in the area, they also practised all kinds of trading and crafts associated with farming. The main destination for farm produce was of course the Roman market, especially after the return of the pope and the Curia. But the Jews also attended the seasonal fairs in the area, at Fara and Magliano. In this economically modest province, the Jews seemed to play a role of broker between the countryside and the city for all kinds of activity, partly because of their relative mobility. In just a few years they became accustomed to moving to new towns in the area, their own place being taken by other Jewish families.

It is to this background of the Jewish participation in all kinds of economic activity that the dispute on usury broke out here, as in other areas. The reasons for the dispute must be sought in questions of rivalry and competition, without of course neglecting the religious differences.

At the end of the 13th century many Jewish communities were expelled from the Kingdom of Naples and probably sought refuge in the southern provinces of Lazio (then Campagna and Marittima) and in the area of the Castelli Romani. This migratory wave joined up with the Roman current of Jewish moneylenders, who at that time were seeking new markets for their capital. Unfortunately the lack of 14th-century archive documents (except for a few sporadic mentions) means we are unable to outline a picture of these settlements until the following century, when the sources became relatively abundant: papal documents, notarial deeds, reforms, communal and provincial account books and statutes. These documents combined indicate a stable presence especially in the Campagna towns (Anagni, Alatri, Ferentino and Veroli), Pontecorvo, Sermoneta, Cori, Fondi, Terracina, Segni, Sezze and Supino, while tiny groups (at times only one household) are recorded at Frosinone, Castro, Maenza and many other places. There were larger groups at Marino, Tivoli, Genazzano, Cave, and Velletri. When Giacomo di Acquasparta was named collector of the 'twentieth' (a five per cent tax introduced at the time of Augustus) from Jews residing in these provinces, the act appointing him included a list of Jewish people in the area, with the taxes to be paid by each household. We thus know the distribution of Jews in the whole area, and we may also form a picture of their economic situation, which appears to have been relatively comfortable. Like the Jews in the other Lazio provinces, these families appear to have been mobile. Proof comes from the changes between this list compiled in 1472 and a similar list drafted in 1476. The towns are usually the same, but some names are not confirmed and others are mentioned for the first time. The statutes in various communes included laws to govern the Jewish community (evidently characterised, albeit in a fluctuating way, by a continuous settlement, although not necessarily composed of the same individuals). In territories subject to the Church the influence of Canon Law was crucial, with its restrictions and traditions, which, however, do not appear to have been applied systematically. The statutory laws themselves, although similar in content are often different in tone. Thus at Anagni, for example, there seems to have been no hostility towards Jews. The same cannot be said for Veroli and Ferentino.

In the last decade of the 15th century Jews began to arrive in the whole area from central and northern cities, like Mantua, Siena, Pescia and Cortona, thus strengthening links with northern Jewish moneylenders.

At the turn of the 16th century, there were new arrivals in the areas near the border with the Kingdom of Naples. The Sicilian Jews, who were expelled from the island in 1492, made their way up from southern Italy in search of a new home. They were repressed by a series of measures in the 16th century which ultimately also eliminated the Jewish presence from the Kingdom of Naples. On their way to the final destination of Rome, the Sicilian and southern Italian Jews sought temporary refuge at Fondi, Cori and Sezzi, where in the first half of the 16th century their presence is documented by notarial and judicial deeds.

These were to be the last years of relative tranquillity. In 1555 Pope Paul v, with the bull *Cum nimis absurdum*, sanctioned the creation of the ghetto in Rome and the beginning of the era of the segregation of Jews from Christians. These restrictions were then extended – with varying degrees of zeal – to all the papal territories. But then in 1569 Pope Pius iv, with the *Hebraeorom gens* bull, decreed that all Jews resident in the State of the Church had to abandon their houses and gather in the ghettos of Rome and Ancona. This decree had dramatic consequences. Over fifty communities disappeared and 115 synagogues were closed in Lazio, Umbria, the Marches and Emilia, bringing to an end hundreds of years of history. There was only to be a short-lived return in 1586, permitted by Sistus v, but then revoked by his successor. Except for special 'commercial permits' granted in the 17th and 18th centuries, it was only after the unity of Italy in the 19th century that the Jews, by then all Romans, were able to return to the localities in the Lazio and, in keeping with the historic tradition, attend all the fairs and markets in the region.

After the brief interlude of freedom under the French occupation and the initial clemency shown by Pope Pius ix at the beginning of his papacy, the Church once more pursued a severe policy towards Jews. Some did, however, manage to stay on (with a series of temporary permits) in the towns where they had set up shop again. In 1853 there were Jews in Bracciano, Campagnano, Frascati, Monterotondo, Nepi, Zagarolo, Civitavecchia, Frosinone, Anagni, Alatri, Priverno, Vallecorsa, Acquapendente and Viterbo. Various sources also indicate they were present at Rieti, Soriano del Cimino, Cori, Veroli, Carpineto Romano and Civita Castellana, where in 1833 a certain Giacobbe Treves took up residence.

From the end of the 19th and the beginning of the 20th century, 'travelling' Jews once more became a regular presence, as they took their wares to the towns and villages of Lazio. Their 'specialities' were rural clothes (i.e. clothes for farm work), often made in their own family workshops in the old ghetto.

The Castelli area was a destination for day trips, honeymoons or holidays. The horizons for Roman Jews, once so willing to travel, was now very limited. There is a tale of a Roman Jew who took his bride on a honeymoon to the panoramic belvedere of Frascati and whispered in Roman Jewish dialect with a sweeping gesture towards Rome in the distance: *Stère mia, ngkaina com'è grande lo ngkolàmme!* ('Esther my dear, look how big the world is!').

*Funerary inscription of Donatos
Grammateus in the synagogue of the
Vernacoli, Catacomba di Monteverde
(Archivio Musei Vaticani; photo by
Archivio Musei Vaticani)*

Bas relief on the Arch of Titus

The sources for this period of history are by now often oral: the testimonies and memories of the guests in the Jewish Community home for the elderly in Rome.

One last terrible chapter was written during the Second World War. In those dramatic years, some Jewish families fleeing from the manhunt triggered off by the roundup of 16 October 1943, sought refuge outside Rome. Their hiding places were mainly in the Castelli area (at Albano and Frascati) and many Jews wishing to enlist in the resistance also arrived in this area. The partisans included Marco Moscati, killed in the Fosse Ardeatine and Pino Levi Cavaglione, a Genoa Jew, who first came to Rome and then went to join the combatants in the Castelli area. He wrote some of the most interesting descriptions of the partisan war in the province of Rome.

JEWS IN ROME

The Jews are arguably the only inhabitants of Rome who can claim an uninterrupted presence in the city for over two thousand years. The banks of the Tiber were the site of the earliest Jewish settlement in Italy and one of the earliest communities in Europe.

The first records of official contacts between Jerusalem and Rome dates back to the ambassadors sent by the Maccabees from 161 BCE to establish an alliance with the Romans against the Seleucid domination. A Jewish community had already permanently settled from the second to the first century BCE. Like the Greeks and the Phoenicians, they were mostly merchants or freed slaves. The original nucleus grew with the arrival of prisoners brought to Rome from 63 to 61 BCE, following Pompey's campaigns in Judaea. Low reliefs on the Arch of Trajan depicting the emperor's triumphal procession with the seven-branched candelabra and the furnishings plundered from the Temple document the conquest of Jerusalem in 70 BCE, following a war began by Vespasian and concluded by his son. This marked the beginning of the Jewish Diaspora in the Roman Empire and the coin *Judaea capta*, minted for the occasion recalls the loss of national independence.

With the arrival of the slaves brought by Titus and then a large number of exiles, the city became the most important community of the Diaspora. There were around 50,000 Jews in ancient Rome, almost ten per cent of the total population. Vespasian imposed a tax – the *fiscus judaicus* – on all Jews in Roman territory, a tax of half a shekel per capita, significantly replacing the offering normally sent to the Temple of Jerusalem with a tribute for the Temple of Jupiter Capitolinus.

A fragmentary picture of Jewish life in imperial Rome emerges from the writings of Latin authors, the Talmud and the inscriptions in the catacombs. Having arrived in various waves, the mass of Jews lived scattered in different quarters of the city: Trastevere, Campus Martius, Porta Capena, Subura, the Esquiline. They were mostly traders or craftsmen. But there were also men of learning, physicians and experts of the Talmud, such as Mattia ben Heresh, who was the director of an important school of Jewish studies (*yeshivah*) in the 2nd century. Twelve synagogues are documented and their names alluded to Roman protectors, their position or provenance of their members: for example, the Augustensi, Agrippensi, Vernacoli, Campensi and Elea.

The Jews were grouped in communities not unlike the modern ones: an organised microcosm with social responsibilities, official representatives, masters or rabbis and even a few important female officials, such as the *mater synagogae*. Archaeological finds from the Ostia synagogue and catacomb decorations reveal that their artistic output was similar to the Roman style of the period.

Judaism was one of the many religions in the imperial melting pot of cultures. The Romans' overall attitude towards the Jews was one of tolerance. To the Latin authors, their customs were superstitions or the strange rites of a sect. Thus, like most Romans, Ovid and Tibullus believed in omens and considered Saturday an unlucky day, *nefas*, because the Jews did not travel on it. Tacitus and Juvenal saw the Sabbath rest as a form of laziness, believing the Jews fasted because they were not to be seen cooking. The Jews' relation with the authorities underwent many vicissitudes. Julius Caesar exempted the Jews from military service, allowing them to profess their religion freely and, according to Suetonius, they expressed their gratitude by participating in the mourning at his funeral. They received similar protection from Augustus, but under Tiberius 4,000 young conscripts were sent to Sardinia by Sejanus, the influential prefect of the Praetorian Guard, as he was anxious to curb the presence of Oriental-origin religious minorities in Rome. Following the *impulsore Chresto* uprisings, at a time when Judaism and Christianity were not yet clearly distinguished, some groups were expelled by Claudius in 49 CE. But later emperors never persecuted the Jews with the violent methods they applied to the followers of the new religion.

In 40 CE Philon of Alexandria arrived in Rome to try and persuade Caligula, who had ordered that his statue be raised in the Temple of Jerusalem, not to exact religious taxes from Jews. Around 80 CE an important delegation of rabbis led by Rabban Gamliel visited the Roman Jews. The Jewish cult was further curbed under Domitian, who feared proselytism and during Hadrian's rule, when circumcision and the study of the Torah were banned.

Meanwhile in Judaea, Jewish life was on its last legs. After putting down the insurrection led by Simon bar-Kokhba in 132 CE, Hadrian razed the Temple and changed the name of Jerusalem to *Aelia Capitolina*. The stifling of the Jewish identity in Palestine did not hinder the spread of spiritual and cultural activities in the Diaspora and Jewish life in Rome was to revive. In this period illustrious rabbis like Shimon bar-Yochai and Eliezer bar-Yose came to the city and played an important role in avoiding new persecutions. Despite banning proselytism, Antoninus Pius allowed the Jews to profess their religion again and to hold public office. But it was only with Caracalla in 212 CE that they were to obtain Roman citizenship, granted to all free men in the empire.

The situation began to change radically with conversion of Constantine to Christianity in 312 and the edict of Milan, making Christianity the official religion of the empire. The Council of Nicaea in 325 definitively separated the two religions. Instead of Saturday, Sunday was established as the day of rest and Christians were not allowed to celebrate Easter at the same time the Jews celebrated Passover nor attend synagogues. This marked the beginning of a policy of restraint and prohibitions, and not only at religious level. The Jews were declared ineligible to testify and their property was confiscated. They were excluded from the army and public office and were not allowed to have slaves.

After the gradual conversion of the Roman Barbarian kingdoms, in the 6th and 7th century, the Jews were practically the only non-Christian community to survive. They are mentioned for the first time in edicts as 'a wicked sect, contaminated people' who follow a 'perverse doctrine'. The codices of Theodosius and Justinian already outline the policy that the popes would pursue in the coming centuries: protect Jewish community life within Christian society, albeit at the same time creating a barrier to limit their freedom of expression. Accordingly, in the collective imagination the Jews began to take on a role full of the symbolic values attributed to them by the Church, even though the restrictive measures were not always applied with the same rigour and did not prevent daily exchanges between Jews and Christians, or the relations between the two cultures – Rome is a good example – and the presence of Jewish settlements in the towns and cities.

The Roman Jews are mentioned in the *Epistles* by Pope Gregory the Great (590-604). Following a request for protection, in the *Sicut Judaeis* bull, the pope established the principle that they could profess their own religion and re-established their right to own property, believing that they should be converted with persuasion and not force. In the period until the 11th century there are few documents mentioning Jews in Rome, by then a tiny minority of a total population reduced to around 40,000 people exhausted by poverty, invasions and devastation. But by the 11-12th century there was a more stable political and economic administration of the city, accompanied by fresh developments in Jewish life. As evidenced by place names, such as *Ruga Judeorum*, the Jewish street near the Church of Santa Cecilia, Trastevere continued to be an important Jewish settlement. The institutions of the community were concentrated in this area: the synagogues, including the temple in Vicolo dell'Atleta, the rabbinical tribunal and the cemetery, situated in the area between the church of San Salvatore a Ripa and Porta Portese.

After a trip to Rome in the 1260s, Benjamin of Tudela described a very lively and culturally active community of around 200 Jews (heads of households) holding respectable positions in city life and, as a consequence, exempt from taxes: craftsmen, tradesmen, Talmud scholars, poets, men of letters, physicians and trusted papal administrators. Among them was the nephew of a rabbi, the lexicologist Nathan ben Yechiel, the author of the Talmud compendium *Sefer 'Arukh* ('Ordered Book') and a contemporary of Kalonimos ben Shabbatai, a master of the Talmud who left Rome for Worms to run the prestigious local school of rabbinical studies.

In the 13th century the Jews gradually moved to the other bank of the Tiber, beyond the *Pons Judeorum* ('Jewish Bridge'). In previous centuries this area had been occupied by groups of tradesmen and craftsmen summoned and protected by noble families living round the Portico of Ottavia and the Theatre of Marcellus. Here, too, there was a *Ruga Judeorum*, later to become the Via Rua del Ghetto, linking the area in front of the Roman theatre with the *Platea Judea*, another Jewish quarter in the area.

At this time Jewish cultural activity and output reached new heights with the *Scriptorum* run by the Anaw, one of the longest-standing Roman Jewish families, like the De Rossi, De Pomis, and the Del Vecchio, with their branches the Piattelli and Delli Mansi. The *Scriptorum* was a genuine workshop with patrons, translators and copyists, including a woman, Paola the daughter of the celebrated amanuensis Avraham ha-Sofer. This group recovered and spread rare codices of Jewish knowledge, and Islamic and Greek culture, thus establishing an important cultural bridge between East and West. In their work they were aided by a group of learned men, philosophers, scientists and literati, including the poet Immanuel Romano, a friend of Busone da Gubbio and Cino da Pistoia and a contemporary of Dante, whom he imitated in a poem written in erudite Hebrew entitled *Machbaroth*.

The principles of segregation and limits to Jewish life established by the Church were more rigorously applied under the rule of Pope Innocent III. In 1215 the Lateran Council imposed the obligation for Jews to wear a badge on their clothes and banned them from holding public office. The fervent Jewish studies attracted the popes' attention to the importance for Jews not only of the Bible (*Tanach*) but also of the Talmud. In 1239 Gregory IX ordered the Talmudic texts to be confiscated as they were considered heretical and failed to conform with Christian doctrine. The first bonfires in Rome marked the beginning of a policy that was to strike deep blows to Jewish culture in the following centuries.

At the end of the 13th century, when the Holy See was in exile in Avignon, Rome was plunged into a crisis as it became a stage for the political struggles and contrasts between foreign nobles and sovereigns bent on taking power. A few hundred Jews, money-changers and moneylenders began to leave Rome for small towns in Lazio and

Parchment manuscript of the
Pentateuch, Arles, 1203 (Biblioteca
della Comunità ebraica, Rome)

INTRODUCTION

central and northern Italy, where capital was in demand to meet the various needs of the communes expanding at both political and economic level. In the *Codex Balduini Trevirensis* Jews are included in the procession to greet Henry VII of Luxembourg in Rome in 1312. Dressed in pointed headgear, the *Pileus cornutus*, they presented the sovereign with a scroll of the Torah. Among the taxes they had to pay was a tribute for the coronation of the emperor.

Like the rest of the population, the Roman Jewish community was diminished and impoverished by the 1348 plague. It was also tainted by the spread of stereotyped anti-Jewish prejudices, which in Rome, as elsewhere in Europe, blamed Jews for the contagion and the crisis in the city. On Pope Martin V's return journey from exile, he met delegations of Jews and from 1419 to 1421 granted them freedom to worship and practice all economic activities. Moreover, he reduced the tax pressure on Roman Jews but established that the tax of 1130 florins for the carnival games should also be levied from Jews resident in the provinces of the Papal States. Although the obligation to wear a badge continued, Martin banned all molestation and forced baptisms. But under the influence of the Spanish monarchy, his successor Eugene IV re-introduced religious, social and economic restrictions, adding another which was to take effect in the next century: the bull *Dudum ad nostram audentiam* established that Jews would have to live *infra certum viculum seu locum a christianis separati*, that is in a ghetto, segregated from Christians. The imminent danger of this measure being applied was warded off by rabbis at the Congress of Tivoli in 1442. They managed to have the measure annulled in exchange for massive sums of money. But by the second half of the century several signals suggested that the anti-Jewish ideological climate was worsening: the Franciscans' preaching to encourage conversion and their attacks on usury often leading to riots, the creation of the Spanish Inquisition (1479) and the accusation of ritual killings by Jews in Trent (1475). In the papal city, however, the full effect of the bull had not yet been felt. Under Pope Sistus IV (1471-84) the composition of the Jewish community began to change with the arrival of many *forenses* (foreigners): French, German and Spanish Jews who had arrived from the Roman countryside and papal cities. These heterogeneous groups integrated into city life, but according to the documents they occupied a subordinate economic position to most Christians, except for the roles played, as always, by physicians and papal archiaters.

After 1492, following the expulsions from Spain, Navarre, Portugal and Sicily, large numbers of Jews went to settle in Rome, where the same popes who had given the Torquemada Inquisition carte blanche, allowed them to live in controlled settlements in the city. The population of the Roman Jewish community almost doubled with the arrival of the largest Italian Sephardic group. The *Descriptio urbis* of 1526 recorded 373 Jewish families, making a total of 1,772 individuals out of the city population of 54,000. Some of the exiles, like the

Catalans, had the means to acquire a house from the Cenci to provide a dignified home for their *scola* (whose transfer was authorised by Pope Leo x in 1519) and to construct a precious marble *aron* (the ark for the scrolls of the Law) in 1523. The Castilians, Aragonese, French, Germans and Sicilians organised independently from the Roman Jews. They settled in the Mercatello area, in the part of the *Platea Judea* later to be called Piazza delle Cinque Scole, where in the 15th century the *Scola Tempio* – the synagogue of the Roman Jews – had been built.

There were frequent and fierce internal conflicts between the original Jewish nucleus and the newcomers from various countries due to differences in outlook, customs, traditions and cultures. In 1524 the banker Daniel da Pisa was summoned to settle a number of disputes and in the *Capitoli* ('Chapters'), approved by Pope Clement VII, he established the administrative principles for the Jewish community, whose official positions were to be equally divided between foreign and Roman Jews.

At the end of the 15th century and in the early decades of the 16th century the Jewish community revived from the demographic, economic and cultural points of view. Integration was fostered by the fact that different Jews lived in the same quarter, and by the use of the Roman dialect as the lingua franca between Jews and in relations with Christian society. Notarial deeds reveal that the Jewish institutions in Trastevere were still active. Under popes who encouraged humanistic learning, like Julius II and the members of the Medici family, Leo X and Clement VII, the grammarian Elia Ha-Levi – friend and Cabbala master of Cardinal Egidio from Viterbo – published his works in Rome in 1518. Hebrew texts had been printed in Rome since the end of the 15th century. Among the most authoritative figures in the community were the philosopher, physician and Pentateuch commentator, Obadia Sforno, and the poet and physician Josef Zarfati. Around this time two men inspired by Messianic aspirations also passed through Rome and asked for the support and protection of Clement VII: David Reubeni pursued the dream of freeing Jerusalem from the Turks and taking the Jews back to the Promised Land, while Salomon Molcho, a Marrano disciple of Reubeni inspired by Cabbala studies was only met with a lukewarm response from the Roman Jews and he ended his days in Mantua at the hands of the Inquisition.

The sack of Rome in 1527 deeply affected the Jewish community, along with the rest of the city, causing impoverishment and a drop in population. Some of the *scole* were forced to unite – the Catalan with the Aragonese and the Castilian with the French – while others simply closed. Under Pope Paul III (1534-49), who convened the Council of Trent, the Counter-Reformation climate and the struggle against heresy spread throughout Italy. In 1542 the Holy Office began its activities in Rome. This also marked the beginning of the conversion campaigns waged by the Church. They encouraged Jews to convert by offering privileges, while conversion centres for neophytes and

*The ghetto in G. B. Falda's
map of Rome, 1676*

B. Picart, The Jews Homage to
the newly-elected Pope, *1721*

catechumens were opened in the Mercatello area and on the Capitol. To pay for the upkeep of these centres, in 1554 Julius III levied a tax of 10 gold ducats from every synagogue in the Papal States. The previous year, during the Jewish New Year, the burning of the Talmud in Campo dei Fiori was a sinister harbinger for the oppression of Jewish culture, and subsequently of the Jewish people.

On 14 July 1555, with the *Cum nimis absurdum* bull, Pope Paul IV created the ghetto, following the example of the compulsory quarter for Jews set up in Venice in 1516. The Rome ghetto, however, was characterised by unprecedented Counter-Reformation intransigence: 'since it is absurd and utterly inconvenient that the Jews, who through their own fault were condemned by God to eternal slavery, can, with the pretext that they are protected by Christian love and tolerated amongst us, show such ingratitude towards Christians and affront them by asking for their mercy... and since we have learned that in Rome and other places they have become so bold as to venture not only to live amongst Christians but also near churches without wearing any distinctive clothing'. The underlying reasoning was equally as violent as the measures, meticulously listed in fifteen points: the Jews had to live in separate quarters with gates; they could not have more than one synagogue; they must sell all their property to Christians; they could not employ Christian servants; they had to wear a badge; and, as economic activities, they could only practice fixed-rate moneylending and the craft of *strazzariae seu cenciariae* – the rag trade. But it took the Roman Jews the whole century to adapt to the new situation. The *scole* were reduced to five (the Tempio, Catalana, Castigliana, Siciliana and Nova) and housed in the same building. The shops and houses outside the *claustrum* were gradually abandoned.

When Pope Pius V forced the Jews to gather in Rome and Ancona in 1566 and 1596, excluding them from all other papal cities, life in the ghetto began to suffer from the effects of overcrowding. In 1593, with the bull *Caeca et obdurata*, Pope Clement VIII confirmed the expulsion, but added Avignon as an additional place of compulsory residence. The greatest pressure was exerted by the Church on the religious front in 1577 when Pope Gregory VIII, continuing the work of Pope Paul III, gave fresh impetus to the conversion campaigns by forcing Jews to listen to sermons and by building the College of the Neophytes. A further step was taken by Urban VIII when the House of the Catechumens was opened near the church of the Madonna dei Monti in 1634. By the end of the 16th century the population had almost doubled compared to the around 1,750 Jews enclosed in 1555. In 1586 Sistus V allowed the Jews to extend the enclosure along the Tiber and granted the expelled the right to return and live 'in the cities, large castles and lands, but not the villas and villages', and to practise any profession, craft or trade, including silk working, a craft widespread among Jews in southern Italy in previous centuries (hence the Roman Jewish surname Della Seta – meaning 'of silk'). This alternation of measures according to the policy of each individual pope characterised the Church's stance from the Middle Ages to the end of the ghetto. There was a continuous, close but ambivalent relation between the pope and the Jews. It was based on safeguarding the Jewish presence as the 'people of testimony', who were economically useful and required a certain protection. On the other hand, the Church policy was based on the principle of separating and limiting Jewish social, economic and religious life, insofar as it was inconceivable that a non-Christian community should live freely and prosper in the papal city. Nonetheless, the Roman Jews considered the pope to be their sovereign. They turned to him for protection, justice and to appeal against severe measures. Similarly, being closed in the ghetto did not preclude contacts between Christians and Jews during the day, when the gates were open.

Since the 12th century the Roman Jews had had to make acts of homage to every newly elected pope on the route from St Peter's to St John Lateran. The rabbi and community representatives had to offer a scroll of the Law (Torah) as a sign of submission, while the crowd jeered and lashed out at them. These gestures did not even cease when the homage was replaced by greetings, accompanied by festoons and well-wishing placards raised along the route by inhabitants of the ghetto. Another crucial time for Roman Jews was Carnival. The rules of the games at Agone and Testaccio established that the competitors should ride on Jews instead of horses, while later descriptions relate how a Jew in a nailed barrel was rolled down from the hill of Testaccio. Although replaced by a tax of 1,130 florins, the *ludi carnascialeschi* were revived in Via Lata, later called Via del Corso. Here the pope attended the spectacle from the Palazzo Venezia: 'the race of Barbarians, buffaloes, donkeys and Jews'. By 1583 there were only 'biped beasts' who ran naked past the mocking populace. The annual proclamations to the effect that the Jews should not be molested or disturbed had little effect. In 1668 Pope Clement IX abolished the race, replacing it with a tribute of 300 scudi to decorate the street and the obligation for community representatives to come to the Capitol and pay homage to the *Conservatori*, remaining bowed until the most senior ordered them to 'go', while the population mocked along the route, often provoking scuffles.

The Community archives contain a letter of 1784, accompanied by a medical certificate from Rabbi Laudadio Modigliani begging the *Conservatori* to be exempted 'from having to be present next Carnival Saturday on the Capitol, so as not to further acerbate my health'. But it was economic difficulties of daily life more than the public humiliation, which made life in the ghetto so harsh. Survival depended on the ability to adapt to circumstances. In the 17th century moneylending fell into decline. In 1682 Pope Innocent XI abolished Jewish loan-banks and in the early 18th century of the original fifty some bankers only three were left. Pawnshops did survive, however.

The roster for collecting bread tax, Scola Siciliana, 1777 (Archivio Comunità ebraica, Rome)

The characteristic crafts of the ghetto developed on the basis of the lacunas in the restrictions reaffirmed several times since Pope Paul IV's bull up to the edict of Pope Pius VI in 1775. In a list of 1726 there were tailors, saddlers, leather craftsmen, traders of carpets, corals and fabrics, travelling salesman, rags and used clothes merchants, menders and embroiderers. The economic hardship was aggravated by the heavy tax burden for Jews. Taxes included not only all the tributes paid by every citizen on bread, meat, wine and salt – often increased for Jews – but also direct or substitute tributes for oppressive measures and a special tax on capital introduced by Gregory XIII in 1577, which the 'University of Jews' (as the community was called) raised by taxing every head of household. In 1668 only 200 out of a total 800 families were able to contribute, while the rest of the ghetto population struggled to survive at subsistence level. In these dire straits the Community became irrecoverably indebted and was practically forced to declare itself bankrupt. In a brief of 30 April 1698 Innocent XII (1691-1700) made the far from surprising comment that the Community 'had reached the point where it could no longer hope to provide in some way for the faithful, nor escape complete ruin'.

The ghetto was one of the most unhealthy quarters in the city, and its wretched condition was worsened by natural calamities: famine, the Tiber flood of 1647, and the plague of 1656. The spread of the disease, circumscribed by the Jews who had promptly set up a quarantine hospital, was described by the physician Rabbi Jacob Zahalon: 'the plague also struck the Jews, who, however, recovered quicker than the Christians. The disease lasted nine months in the ghetto and 800 people, adults and children, died. At that time the Jewish population was 4,127 souls.'

Jewish cultural life seems to have been restricted and stifled in all fields – Hebrew studies, philosophy and literature. There were some rare exceptions, however, such as the poetess Deborah Ascarelli, who in the early 16th century translated into Italian the works of the Hebrew poet Mose da Rieti, or the astronomer and scientist Sabato Ambron, the author of *Pancosmosophia*. One night in April 1753 the Holy Office requisitioned all Hebrew books in the ghetto and loaded them onto thirty-eight carts. After considerable pleading by the Community and careful examination, only a few biblical texts and prayer books were returned, albeit censored in the places considered to be in contrast with Christian teachings.

One very special figure was Rabbi Tranquillo Vita Corcos (1659-1730), a physician, Cabbalist, and expert on the Classical world and Hebrew culture. He was one of the few intellectuals in his time able to debate on an equal footing with the papal authorities. A member of the *Congrega dei Sessanta*, the administrative council of the Jewish community, Corcos wrote many memorials to the pope, describing the shocking situation in the ghetto, and apologetic writings to defend Jews from continuous confiscations made on the grounds of unfounded provocative accusations, such as that of ritual murder. In these writings he stressed the importance of Hebrew texts in the Christian tradition.

Given the precarious conditions of life, the ghetto had its own internal organisations to meet any emergencies: the *Università* and its administrative structures maintained official relations with the papacy, while the *Cinque Scole* was the place of prayer, study and meeting. Thirty confraternities dealt with all kinds of social, cultural and religious activities: from dowries for poor girls to running the cemeteries, from educating the young to assisting the old. One confraternity, the *Yerushalaim*, had the task of sending the obols to Israel, thus keeping the centuries-old relation between Rome and Jerusalem alive.

The Roman Jews were not slow to respond to the ideas of equality and liberty championed by the French Revolution. When the Napoleonic troops arrived in Rome and the Roman Republic was proclaimed in 1798-99, many inhabitants of the ghetto were quick to enrol in the civic guard and raised the Tree of Liberty in Piazza delle Cinque Scole. They hailed their emancipation in the law stating that 'Jews, who meet all the conditions required for Roman citizenship, will only be subject to the laws common to all Roman citizens'.

But emancipation for the Jews of Rome was still a long way off. On 14 January 1814 the French abandoned the city and a few days later Pope Pius VII returned in a climate of complete restoration. In 1823 under Pope Leo XII a small extension to the ghetto was granted to include the urban block of Via della Reginella. But by now those few families who could afford it began to move to Tuscany and Lombardy-Veneto in search of better fortune.

By now, however, liberal public opinion in Rome and abroad had begun urging the pope to improve the living conditions of the Jews. Gregory XVI had several meetings with Rabbi Sabato Beer and Samuele Alatri, a liberal-minded intellectual who was in contact with the most representative figures of European Jewry. He was to lead the Roman community towards emancipation, while the Rothschild bankers, who had boosted the papal finances with a loan, demanded the abolition of the ghetto in no uncertain terms.

Great hopes of reform were placed in Pope Pius XI, who at the beginning of his papacy, introduced measures to ease the hardship of the Jews. Bread or money was often distributed and forced attendance of sermons and homages at the Capitol were suppressed. In 1847 Massimo D'Azeglio, one of the leaders of emancipation, described the situation of Roman Jews: 'families of these wretched people live at times more than twelve to a room, heaped up with no distinction of sex, or state of health on every floor, in the attics and even in underground holes, which in more fortunate dwellings are used as cellars. But even this fails to describe the ghetto, or a minimal part of the hardship, which in the silence and neglect of ignored poverty are to be found between its walls.' Considerable help also came from a

Houses in the ghetto in Via della Fiumara overlooking the Tiber; in the background is the bridge called Ponte Quattro Capi and the Isola Tiberina, 1886 (Archivio fotografico comunale)

Roman popular leader – Angelo Brunetti called Ciccruacchio. In 1847 he organised a demonstration of solidarity in favour of the Jews, involving over 2,000 Romans. On 17 April 1848, on the eve of the Passover marking the freedom from slavery in Egypt, Pope Pius IX ordered the gate and walls of the ghetto to be pulled down to the triumphant acclaim of the population. Definitive equality with the other citizens eventually came with advent of the Republic of Mazzini, Saffi and Armellini in 1849. At this time Roman Jews had their first contacts with several Jewish patriots who had come to the city from other regions to support the democratic regime. Among those in Garibaldi's entourage were Giacomo Venezian and Ciro Finzi, who both lost their lives fighting for the cause. When Pope Pius IX returned to the city, the Jews were again forced to reside in the ghetto, albeit without gates, and were once more subject to the previous taxes. In 1864 there was a case of kidnapping for a forced conversion, similar to the Mortara case in Bologna in 1858. This time the victim was an eleven-year-old cobbler's apprentice called Giuseppe Coen.

Following Carlo Alberto's example in Piedmont, the emancipation of the Jews followed the developments of the Risorgimento and the unity of Italy. But the Roman ghetto remained the last emblematic legacy of discrimination in a period of liberal and democratic principles. The storming of the Porta Pia on 20 September 1870 marked the end of the temporal power of the pope, the definitive abolition of the ghetto and full equality for Roman Jews with other citizens. An interesting sign of the times came when Samuele Alatri was elected city councillor and then a member of parliament.

The first decades of freedom were anything but easy for the Roman Jews. Very few had the means to pursue university studies, exercise the previously prohibited professions or open fabrics shop outside the ghetto. They thus lagged behind the rising Italian bourgeoisie. Most Jews were still small shopkeepers, travelling salesman or rag and bone merchants or were involved in businesses linked to the activities in the centuries of imposition or repression. They had problems of identity and integration into city life as they gradually abandoned the ghetto, by now uninhabitable due to decay. It was completely destroyed from 1886 to 1904, in accordance with the new urban plan for the Italian capital. But the Community had to make up for the collapse of the self-sufficient microcosm that the ghetto had been. In 1883 the *Università* worked out a statute, reorganising its structure in keeping with the times to include elected positions and subscriptions. The old confraternities were fused to give rise to the *Deputazione centrale israelitica di carità*, the first core of the current social services. With the opening of the temple, built on the area of the demolished ghetto and visible from all the city's panoramic viewpoints, Roman Jewry took on a new image in 1904. It was also to boast a high-ranking politician in mayor Ernesto Nathan in 1907.

In 1938 the 'Laws for the Defence of the Race', introduced by the fascist regime, caught the Jewish community unprepared, since after the Jewish participation in the First World War they had been completely integrated into city and national life. In Rome the sudden exclusion from work, school and public office immediately conjured up spectres from the past, thought to have been definitively laid. In just over a month all kinds of Jewish schools were set up for all levels. They were able to accommodate 600 children and ensured they would continue with their studies, often under the guidance of first-rate teachers, such as the mathematician Guido Castelnuovo, who had been expelled from the universities.

In 1941 the Jews became 'second-class citizens'. This meant another humiliating act of submission to the regime as they were pressed into forced labour along the banks of the Tiber. Few Jews left the city or hid on the arrival of the Nazi troops. They trusted that in Italy and especially in Rome the presence of the Vatican would prevent the arrests and deportations that had taken place in Germany. In September 1943 fifty kilos of gold demanded by Kappler were collected in only thirty-six hours. Over the next few days the SS occupied the Community offices, confiscated registers and documents and plundered the precious and rare codices kept in the library. And this was only the beginning. At dawn on 16 October 1943 special divisions of German police commanded by Theodor Dannecker surrounded the area of the Portico of Ottavia and seized 1,021 men, women, elderly and children. A systematic manhunt began throughout the city which led to the deportation of over 2,000 Jews. Most families were saved thanks to the solidarity of their fellow citizens who risked their own lives to hide them in houses, attics, cellars and country cottages. The parish priests also provided invaluable help as did the monasteries and even the hospitals. The doctors in Fatebenefratelli Hospital invented a new disease to keep the Jews in the safety of the wards – K's disease – alluding to the German general Kesserling. As a reprisal for a partisan attack in Via Rasella, 335 people, including seventy-five Jews, were massacred in the Fosse Ardeatine by the SS on 24 March 1944.

Jews were very active in the resistance in the city and surrounding area. Many young people died for the cause, such as Eugenio and Sylvia Elfer. Two leading figures from contemporary culture, the anti-fascist Jewish intellectuals, Leone Ginzburg and Eugenio Colorni also perished. Another courageous partisan was Enzo Sereni. Of a noted Roman Jewish family, he was a teacher and pioneer in the Zionist-Socialist movement. After leaving his kibbutz in Palestine, he joined the allies in the liberation of Italy and was parachuted beyond the Gothic Line on 15 May 1944. Captured by the Germans, he was killed at Dachau.

The current Jewish community took shape after the war. In the collective effort to reconstruct, a number of institutions were created or revived. Mostly with their roots in the old ghetto confraternities, they became a highly developed network of social, cultural, religious and educational services for a population of around 15,000 Jews.

In 1948 the foundation of the state of Israel, greeted by a festive and symbolic ceremony at the Arch of Titus, strengthened the centuries-old relations between Roman Jews and their historic homeland. In Rome the Jewish society became increasingly pluralistic with the arrival of members of various traditions, such as the Ashkenazim from Central and Eastern Europe and Libyan Jews, who arrived in large numbers after the persecutions in 1956 and 1967. A serious episode of anti-Semitism left a scar on community life on 9 October 1983, when a terrorist attack on the crowd coming out of the synagogue resulted in the death of a child – Stefano Gaj Taché – and forty people being hurt. In a very different atmosphere on 13 April 1986 the Temple witnessed the historic visit of John Paul II. For the first time in Rome a pope prayed together with a rabbi, describing the Jews as 'our elder brothers'.

In a climate of democratic pluralism and the active defence of minorities, the Roman Jewish community continues its more than a thousand-year-old presence in city life, making its voice felt through its public services and lively cultural activities, often pursued jointly with other local and national organisations.

Lake Vico

Lake Bracciano

Civitavecchia

A 12

Tyrrhenian Sea

Itinerary 1
Rome and its province:
Ariccia, Castelnuovo di Porto, Civitavecchia, Frascati, Genazzano, Ostia, Palestrina, Sacrofano, Segni, Tivoli and Velletri.

Rome is the most important centre in the region, and boasts the longest-standing and largest Jewish community in Italy. To make the visit easier, nine itineraries have been suggested. The provincial towns listed can all be easily reached from the capital and may be visited in a few hours.

Castelnuovo di Porto

Sacrofano

Tiber

G.R.A.

Rome

Tivoli

A 24

A I

Palestrina

Genazzano

Frascati

Ostia

Ariccia

Segni

Velletri

A 24

◄ Rome

A I

● Anagni

● Alatri

Veroli ●

● Cori

● Frosinone

● Sermoneta

● Sezze

● Priverno

● Fondi

● Terracina

Tyrrhenian Sea

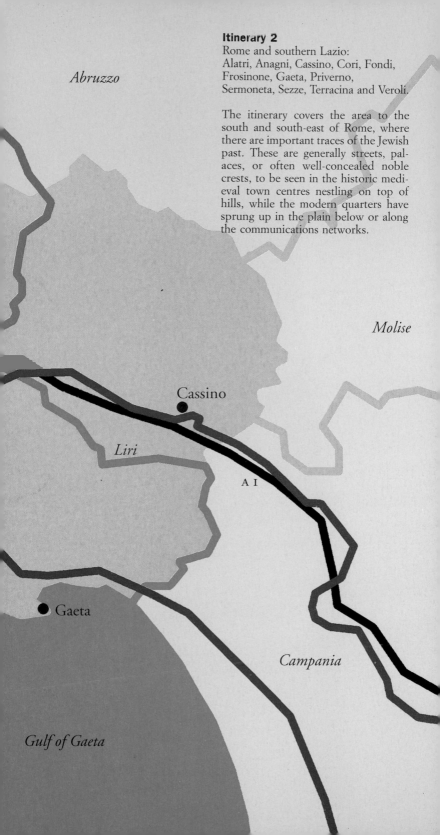

Itinerary 2

Rome and southern Lazio:
Alatri, Anagni, Cassino, Cori, Fondi,
Frosinone, Gaeta, Priverno,
Sermoneta, Sezze, Terracina and Veroli.

The itinerary covers the area to the
south and south-east of Rome, where
there are important traces of the Jewish
past. These are generally streets, palaces, or often well-concealed noble
crests, to be seen in the historic medieval town centres nestling on top of
hills, while the modern quarters have
sprung up in the plain below or along
the communications networks.

Abruzzo

Molise

Cassino

Liri

A I

Gaeta

Campania

Gulf of Gaeta

Tuscany

Lake Bolsena

● Montefiascone

● Tuscania

● Viterbo

Lake Vico

● Tarquinia

Tyrrhenian Sea

A 12

Itinerary 3
Rome and northern Lazio:
Farfa, Montefiascone, Orte, Rieti,
Tarquinia, Tuscania, and Viterbo.

This broad area stretches out to the
north to north-west of Rome and has
many towns with interesting evidence
of the Jewish past. The towns listed are
only some of many and are suggested as
reference points for the traveller.
Throughout the area there was once a
host of small groups. But they disappeared when segregation in the Roman
ghetto became obligatory.

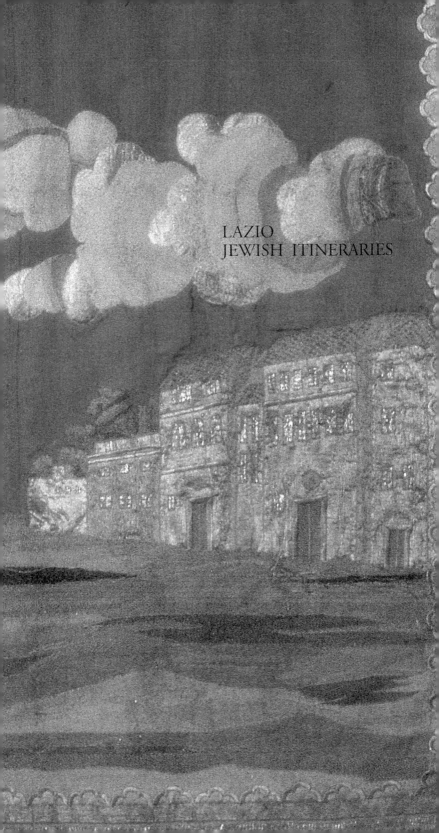

LAZIO
JEWISH ITINERARIES

Alatri

Alatri, the Decarcia Vineri, *now Vicolo Vezzacchi; according to local tradition this was once the Jewish quarter*

Inhabitants 5,800
Altitude 502
Province of Frosinone
Itinerary 2

Situated on the slopes of the Ernici hills, the ancient town of *Alatrium* was a Roman settlement. Today it is mainly a market town for the rural population living scattered in the surrounding countryside. Alatri is a gem of medieval architecture, especially because of its polygon-shaped town walls (two kilometres long and three metres high).

By starting from Piazzale della Libertà, with the war memorial, and going along Via Emanuele Filiberto Duca d'Aosta and then Via Battista, you reach the historic centre round the Piazza Santa Maria Maggiore. At the centre of the square is *Fonte Pia* (a fountain erected to the memory of Pope Pius IX). Round the sides of the square are the 18th-century church of *Santa Maria dei Padri Scolopi*, the medieval *Palazzo Gentili* and the *Liceo* (grammar school – remodelled in various periods), the Neoclassic *Palazzo Comunale* (Town Hall), and alongside the church of *Santa Maria Maggiore* (of Romanesque origin but radically rebuilt in the 15th-century), which lends its name to the square. In all likelihood the synagogue was in this area.

By taking first Via Matteotti and then Corso Vittorio Emanuele – both are lined with medieval buildings – until Via del Duomo, you come to the *Acropolis*, a polygonal construction with a trapezoid-shaped plan. Of the original five entrances only two have survived: the Porta Aeropago (or Maggiore) and the Porta dei

Falli (or Minore). You can walk all the way round the perimeter of the area of the acropolis, which contains the 17th-century cathedral of San Paolo, built over the remains of an ancient Roman temple. The squat bell tower alongside provides access to the bishop's palace.

By going back along Corso Vittorio Emanuele, you come to the church of *San Francesco*. The Gothic portal has survived but the interior was completely remodelled in the 18th century. By continuing along Via San Francesco and turning into Via Cavour, with the Gothic *Palazzo Gottifredi*, now a major exhibition space, you then cross Largo Ricciotti and Via della Repubblica to get back to the starting point in Piazza della Libertà.

In 1499 Rabbi Ruben of Alatri agreed to teach Hebrew to Servo, the brother of Salomone di Sezze, an inhabitant of Sermoneta. This is the first documented piece of information providing evidence of the existence of a Jewish community in Alatri. According to the documents (there are only a few but they contain valuable information), the small community had physicians, rabbis, and Hebrew schools, thus demonstrating a fairly high level of culture. A notarial deed of 1529 reveals that a text by Maimonides and a *Machzor* (prayer book) were sold for five ducats to Rabbi Mele from Alatri. A copy of the town statutes (1549) refers to the local Jews in measures probably dating from the mid-14th century. These measures included the prohibition for Jews to work on Sundays, not so much because they were required to live like Christians, but they were asked to respect the Christian religion.

A tax document of 1472 testifies to the presence of five households at Alatri, including two widows. The life of these families was occasionally marred by quarrels. In 1466 a certain Rosa di Leuccio had a noisy row in the street with an inhabitant from Anagni. And a few years later, in 1499, a wedding degenerated into a fight, instigated by some Roman Jewish guests.

Notarial documents provide information about the synagogue, situated near Piazza Santa Maria Maggiore, where the town hall once stood. According to local tradition the building of the *decaria Vineri*, was in Vicolo Vezzacchi, not far from Piazza Santa Maria Maggiore. Following the bull issued by Pope Pius v in 1569, the Jews were forced to leave the town, and the synagogue building became the property of the podesta of Segni. In 1468 the Alatri Jews were preoccupied with procuring land for a cemetery. They eventually found a lot including an olive grove outside the town walls in the 'Contrada Torre delli Paczi'.

Alatri became a very common surname for Roman Jews (→ Segni/Jewish surnames).

From 1472 to 1476 in the nearby village of **Collepardo** only one Jewish household paid a tribute (five ducats) to Iacobus de Acquasparta, the tax collector of the twentieths from Jews residing in the Papal States. The tax registers record the collection of taxes and indicate the various localities with contributors as early as the 15th century. They are thus one of the main sources of information about the Jewish presence in Lazio.

Anagni

Inhabitants 7,800
Altitude 424 m
Province of Frosinone
Itinerary 2

Situated in a dominant position overlooking the valley of the river Sacco, the ancient settlement of *Anagnia* was once inhabited by the Ernici. The medieval centre offers several attractions for the visitor. It stretches from the Porta Cerere to the Porta Santa Maria, at either end of the Strada Vittorio Emanuele II, the main street running the whole length of the town. In the stretch between Piazza Marconi and Piazza Cavour is the *Barnekow House*, a 14th-century Romanesque edifice (now a museum for the work of sculptor Tommaso Gismondi), and the Romanesque church of *Sant'Andrea* (remodelled in the 18th-century). In Piazza Cavour, the town centre, is the war memorial, while on one side are the steps of the *Parco della Rimembranza* (Memorial Park,), with fine panoramic views.

By continuing along Strada Vittorio Emanuele II, after Piazza Cavour, you come to the 13th-century town hall (rebuilt several times). In the 16th-century a number of local Jewish families lived in this area. Having gone past Piazza Bonifacio VIII and up Via Maggiore, you come to the 13th-century *Palazzo di Bonifacio VII*. A residence for emperors and pope, this palace was the scene for the infamous episode of the 'affront' to Pope Boniface VIII in 1303, when some subjects of Philip V 'the Fair' of France took him prisoner for having excommunicated their sovereign. Dante alludes to the episode in the *Divine Comedy* (Purgatory, Canto XX, 86-93).

The cathedral of *Santa Maria* stands in Piazza Innocenzo III. It was built over an ancient acropolis, also, according to archive sources, the area of the synagogue. Begun in the 11th century, the cathedral was remodelled several times. The twelfth-century Romanesque bell tower is isolated from the main body of the church, containing a number of interesting frescoes. By going along Strada Vittorio you come to Porta Santa Maria. Two panoramic streets parallel to the main thoroughfare run along stretches of the ancient Roman walls and medieval houses right round the whole perimeter of the town back to the starting point.

In 1332 a Jew is mentioned in what to all effects is an official town deed (*civis agnagnius*). In an agreement with the Holy See in 1399 the town asked for the same treatment for resident Jews as for other citizens. The Anagni town statutes had precise rules governing Jewish loans, guaranteeing the bankers a good standard of living, although the usual restrictions did also apply. According to some documents there was a relaxed relationship between Christians and Jews. Not surprisingly, this attracted more Jews to the area – at least five households are documented. The community boasted two famous physicians: Master Ventura, originally from Alatri, and his son Salomone, who was physician to Pope Martin V.

The exact location of the Jewish houses is not known. The only information we have for a house concerns a certain Abramo di Manuele, who lived at the end of 'Via Balney', near the town hall. According to popular tradition, the synagogue was in a building on the right-hand side of the present cathedral.

In nearby **Anticoli Corrado** (→ Cassino), the only evidence of a Jewish presence was the register of taxes paid by Jews in 1550. There were only two contributors, one of them, Michele, had come from **Ceprano**.

Ariccia

Inhabitants 14,000
Altitude 412 m
Province of Rome
Itinerary 1

One of the *Castelli Romani* ('Roman Castles'), the ancient Roman town of *Aricia* is said to take its name from the curls (*ricci*) of the goddess Ceres. Now a small resort and tourist attraction, the town has grown out from the historic centre round *Piazza della Repubblica*. Both the layout and the individual buildings of the square were designed by Gian Lorenzo Bernini (1598-1680). At its centre are two fountains, while along the side is the imposing *Palazzo Chigi* formerly Savelli (the Jews lived nearby), and the round-plan church of *Santa Maria dell'Assunzione*. The presbytery houses a large fresco of the *Assumption* by the French artist Borgognone (1621-75) and works on canvas from the same period.

The Jewish presence in Ariccia seems to date back to Roman times. According to Classical sources, following the expulsion of Jews from Rome at the behest of Claudius, a group of Jews sought refuge in Ariccia and stayed on for around six years. There is no further mention of Jews until 1235, when in the book of baptisms in the church of Santa Maria della Riccia, there is an entry for Lucia, daughter of the Jew Isac.

An 18th-century historian relates that the area in front of Piazza Giudia and below the Palazzo Savelli was still known as the ghetto. On the basis of such place names, the Jewish quarter is thought to have been between the present-day streets of Via Egeria, Via Laziale and Via Silvia.

Ariccia is a common surname among Roman Jews (→ Segni/Jewish surnames).

In nearby **Genzano** the tax register for 1550 only records one Jewish contributor. The same register for the year 1566 no longer has any Jewish names, although there were certainly Jews in the town, since from 1567 to 1583 Jechiel Manoscrivi carried out three circumcisions. It was only in the late 19th century that a small, group of Jews returned to Genzano.

The Jewish community was granted its own burial area (seven white marble tombstones survive) within the town cemetery just outside the town on the provincial road to Nemo.

Cassino

Inhabitants 15,000
Altitude 40 m
Province of Frosinone
Itinerary 2

Cassino is situated on the river Rapido, a tributary of the Liri. The present-day town was completely rebuilt about one kilometre away from the former centre, totally destroyed in one of the longest and most violent battles in the Second World War in Italy (1943-44).

The original Roman settlement, *Casinum* (an allusion to the river Volturno), was situated on the slopes of the hill destined to be the site of the first Benedictine abbey. From 874 to 1863 the town was called San Germano. Very little evidence survives of the ancient centre of Casinum: the *Roman Amphitheatre* (1st century BCE), the *Augustan Theatre*, and the *Baths of Varro* are all located outside the town. In addition to its rural tradition and manufacturing industries, the modern town is also a communications junction between Lazio and Campania. The centre has developed round Piazza De Gasperi, with the town hall and the post office and telephone company buildings. The *Monastery of Monte Cassino* situated on top of a hill nine kilometres from the modern town was completely reconstructed after the long battle of 1943-44, whose violence is attested by the Monte Calvario war cemetery, where 30,000 soldiers are buried, opposite the monastery.

Since the town was completely destroyed in the war, the area inhabited by the Jews cannot be pinpointed. We do know, however, that as early as the 10th century a small Jewish community had settled in the land of St Benedict. A document from this period records a Jewish loan of 500 gold pieces to the monks of the monastery who pawned the altar cloth of St Benedict, which had once belonged to Charlemagne. It was eventually redeemed by Emperor Henry II.

Since the days of Gregory IX, there had been a *judeca* (ghetto) in the town. In 1232 a bull ordered Stefano, the papal chaplain, to grant the monks of Monte Cassino possession of the area, adding that the soldiers of Frederick II be sent away from Badia and Rocca Janula.

In the Jewish quarter the people worked at silk-weaving and dyeing fabrics. For this activity and for butchering animals, they were exempt from taxes but had to dye the cloth for the nuptial bedclothes of the tax collector's daughter. The subdeacon Egidio, the pope's chaplain, ordered shops to be built in the Jewish area. The profits were used to buy tunics for the monks. Any Jews temporarily staying in the town were granted the same privileges as the residents, provided they lodged in the Jewish quarter.

There is no record of the social and juridical conditions of the Jews in the town, but they were generally welcomed as long as they obeyed the laws. The monastery gave them protection, which they had to pay for with taxes and by providing loans.

Along or near the Via Casilina, the major road south, there were small Jewish groups in localities such as **Patrica**, **Castro dei Volsci**, **Vallecorsa**, **Ceprano** and **Pontecorvo**. All paid the twentieth (i.e. five per cent of their income from assets and property), collected by a commissioner appointed by the Apostolic Chamber.

Not far from the monastery, at **Tora e Piccilli,** a forced labour camp was set up from 1940 to 1943 to accommodate all the men from the Naples Jewish community.

Castelnuovo di Porto

Civitavecchia

Inhabitants 4,100
Altitude 250 m
Province of Rome
Itinerary 1

Inhabitants 49,000
Altitude 10 m
Province of Rome
Itinerary 1

Originally a Capena town, Castelnuovo was a feudal possession of the Colonna family in the Middle Ages in the dioceses of Porto, hence the second part of its name. Today this mixed rural and industrial town still has a small historic centre not far from the modern quarters, which have developed along the Via Flaminia. The main square includes the 15th-century *Ducal Palace* (remodelled in the 17th century) and the 19th-century church of *Maria Assunta*, built over an earlier Romanesque church.

From 1563 to 1575 the physician Jechiel Manoscrivi circumcised four boys in this small town. In the 16th century there was a synagogue which paid a tribute of, first, ten and, then, twelve scudi to the House of the Catechumens. There were also at least two loan-banks in the area.

Not far away is **Rignano Flaminio**. Here Jechiel Manoscrivi carried out five circumcisions from 1554 to 1586. This was a time of great movement due to the expulsion of Jews from the smaller towns in the Papal States. Following these upheavals, Shelomo, the son of Jaakov, a resident at Rignano, was granted a licence to open a loan-bank at Castelnuovo di Porto.

In 1588 some Jews were granted a licence for monylending at Rignano.

The original port, built at the behest of the Roman Emperor Trajan (53-117 BCE), was called *Centumcellae* until 889. The current name shared by many Italian towns, refers to the 'old' origins of the town. Now an industrial centre, Civitavecchia owes its fame primarily to its role as a major sea terminal linking the Italian peninsula with Sardinia.

The city grew up round the port, reached from the south by Viale Garibaldi. The large harbour complex is protected by two large structures: to the south the still well-preserved *Walls of Trajan* and, to the north, the *Bastion of Sangallo* and Roman remains along the Vespucci pier enclosing the ancient Roman harbour. The *Fort of Michelangelo* overlooks the southern bight. This rectangular-plan Renaissance construction (82 x 100 m) has four corner towers and an octagonal keep bearing the crest of the Farnese family. Behind the fort, in Largo Plebisciti, the *National Archaeological Museum* is housed in a small palace built by Pope Clement XIII in 1764 to accommodate the command of the garrison and the papal customs offices.

Entered by passing through Largo Cavour, the historic centre consists of the area round Piazza Vittorio Emanuele with the 17th-century cathedral of *San Francesco* (rebuilt after the Second World War). In nearby Piazza Leandra is the church of *Santa Maria Maris Stella*, while in Via

Civitavecchia, the Roman ruins
at the old dockyard

Gabriel D'Annunzio the church of *Santa Maria dell'Orazione* (or della Morte) was remodelled in the 18th-century and has a dome decorated with 19th-century frescoes. By going along the modern Corso Marconi, you come to Piazza Calamatta with its gardens giving onto the port and remains of the medieval *Palazzo della Rocca*, where in 1347 Cola di Rienzo sought refuge after fleeing Rome.

Every August there are a number of traditional folklore festivals in Civitavecchia, including the *Sagra del mare* ('Feast of the Sea').

An ancient Roman funeral epigraph came from 'the Alibrandi vine, at Pozzolano, where the Via Aurelia passed by many old tombs'. The Latin inscription included the names of a Jewish husband and wife: Iulius Iuda and Iulia Maria. This is the earliest evidence of a Jewish presence in Civitavecchia.

More accurate information is available in the Middle Ages. The town statutes of 1451 imposed fines on anyone working on Sundays and feast days, inside or outside Civitavecchia. The fines were larger when the offenders were Jews.

Following the various restrictive papal bulls, many Jews left the port to go and live in quieter areas. From 1556 Giuseppe da Civitavecchia and his sons were living in Mantua, where, with the consent of the Gonzaga, the ruling noble family, they ran a loan-bank.

Around a century later Jews began to return to Civitavecchia to engage in commerce. Anxious to give a fresh impetus to trade in the town, in 1692 Pope Innocent XII invited Jews from the Ancona ghetto to return to Civitavecchia and open a 'shop of public accounting' with a capital of 10,000 scudi. Introducing a similar kind of liberal regime as that in Leghorn, the pope ordered a building with eighty-two rooms and forty attics to be constructed for the newcomers just outside the city in the area called Borgo di Sant'Antonio Abate.

The newcomers soon commanded considerable respect. In 1690 the Roman Jews Abram di Modigliano and Sabato Trionfi won a tender for the duration of over seventy years to supply 300 beds for the soldiers in the city garrison. The contract stipulated that they had to supply 'a mattress of three mesh lengths full of wool, a bolster, a quilt like wool, and two sheets to be changed every month'. On the strength of this important contract, Angelo di Modigliano, son of Abram, applied for a licence to run a loan-bank and the permission to trade in all kinds of goods (the outcome of the application is not known). The Ascarelli brothers also obtained an important order at the end of the 18th century to supply coats and other clothes for the troops. The Ascarelli was the only family allowed to stay on in Civitavecchia, even after the measures abolishing all possible respites for Jews in the territory of the Papal States.

Cori, Porta Ninfina, the entrance to the quarter of the same name in Lower Cori, where the Jews lived

Cori

Inhabitants 10,000
Altitude 384 m
Province of Latina
Itinerary 2

According to legend, the original Roman colony in a Volscian territory was founded by the Trojan Dardanus. The name *Cora*, however, seems to derive from Coras of Argos, who is thought to have rebuilt the town. Nestling in the foothills of the Lepini mountains, today Cori is a market town. It is divided into two separate parts: Cori Valle (220 m) and Cori Alto (398 m). A good place to begin the visit to Cori Valle is the Via della Stazione and the nearby *Oratorio dell'Annunziata* (14th century). The original oratory facade with the town coat-of-arms depicting a rampant lion is still intact, as is a cylindrical tower not far off. Via Accrocca leads to the old medieval centre: from the flat street of Via Ninfina you enter a maze of alleys in a quarter said by some sources to have been the Jewish settlement until the 16th century. By going up a steep stairway on the left, from Via della Collegiata, you come to Piazzale Santa Maria della Pietà, the Renaissance collegiate church square (remodelled several times until the 19th century). By going up from Via Accrocca on the right, you reach Piazza Romana and Via Pelasga, a steeply rising street lined by the historic town walls, made of huge blocks, leading to the remains of the *Temple of Castor and Pollux*. Rebuilt in 89 CE, all that survives of the temple are two Corinthian columns (10 meters high and 1 meter in diameter), supporting a fragment of architrave.

Cori, Via degli Orti, near Via delle Colonne, an area where Jews had shops and houses in the 16th century

By going back the same way and turning into Via Pelasga, you come to Piazza Sant'Oliva. The church of *Sant'Oliva* stands in the square and is made up of two buildings – one medieval, the other 15th-century – joined together and re-modelled several times in the 18th century. Not far from here is the point where Cori Valle meets Cori Alto. A series of avenues rise up alongside stretches of the town walls to Piazza Signina, the centre of Cori Alto. In the square a cylindrical tower, the *Torre di Silla* stands beside many medieval remains. By turning into Via Tempio di Ercole and passing through Piazza Monte Pio, you cross the small well-preserved medieval quarter, also claimed to have been a Jewish settlement (contradicting claims that the Jewish settlement was in Cori Valle). And in fact this area is commonly known as the *ghettarello* – 'little ghetto'. By continuing up the street, you arrive in an open area with the *Temple of Hercules*. Today all that survives of the 1st-century temple are eight columns, part of the Doric trabeation, the pediment and the entrance wall with the portal. There is, however, a splendid view out over the Pontine plain as far as the sea.

Every summer the *Carosello dei rioni* ('Tournament of the Quarters') is held in Cori, featuring groups of *sbandieratori* ('flag-wavers').

Jews certainly already lived in Cori in the 15th century, when Mose, son of Shabbetai of Cori, was granted a permit to travel and trade. They were well integrated into Christian society and there is no mention of friction with the rest of the population. There are only two recorded cases of disputes between Jews and Christians and another two episodes involving rows between Jews. The community was led by a 'prior of the synagogue' and contributed 25 carlini towards the expense of the traditional annual festival of the *Palio di Sant'Oliva*. Although the town statutes included the usual anti-Jewish measures, the

Cori, Piazza dell'Orticara; according to local tradition this was called the ghettarello *('little ghetto') or the* Giudaica *and according to oral tradition one building was known as the synagogue*

Cori, crest with a lily on a building in Piazza dell'Orticara

local authorities protected the Jews' rights. In 1532 three Christians from Velletri were tried by the Curia for having smashed up the shop of two Jews.

The local Jewish community engaged in a wide range of activities. In addition to the usual profession of moneylending, they also traded in silks, copper utensils, wool, and leather. They also owned vineyards and animals, which they often left to be managed by their Christian fellow citizens. Prayers and sacred texts were taught in the synagogue and in one 16th-century document the temple was even described as the *ginnasio* – gymnasium (high school).

With the advent of Pope Paul IV in 1555, the situation changed in Cori, and the small community was forced to yield up its books, which were burnt on a bonfire. This may explain why, in 1566, the Cori Jews enthusiastically responded to the invitation made by Don Joseph Nassi, the great councillor of the Sultan, to move to Tiberias.

Around the same time the Cori Jews had an ominous sign for their future when the man who had murdered Abramo di Bezalel was absolved. In the presence of Rabbi Angelo Gallico di Nepi, an assembly in the synagogue thus decided for a mass move and entrusted four of its members with the organisation of the journey. But for some unknown reason, the exodus never took place. And from 1561 to 1579, Jechiel Manoscrivi, who practised medicine in the towns of central Italy, registered five circumcisions at Cori.

The 1569 edict was applied very late in Cori, since in 1591 there still seems to have been a Jewish loan-bank. After this date, however, there is no more mention of Jews in Cori.

According to notarial documents, the Jews had lived in the Porta Ninfina quarter, in Cori Valle, the lower part of the town. There were many Jewish shops and houses on the Piazza delle Torri (now Piazza Ninfina), the economic and social hub of the quarter. There were, however, also shops and houses in the other three sections of the quarter: Partita Ultima, Partita Columnarum, and the Partita Plagiarum, now the areas adjacent to Piazza Ninfina, Via della Colonne and the church of San Michele Arcangelo. There was also a synagogue in Partita Plagiarum, at least until 1536, when it was sold for 20 ducats to a certain Antonio Colutia. All of the houses had Christian houses next door and so there can be no talk of a concentration in a limited area, and even less of a ghetto. Moreover, the Cori statutes only set one limit to the movement of the Jews: they were not allowed to leave their houses on Holy Friday, except for physicians going to treat the sick. But the documents are strangely contradicted by the local tradition concerning the *ghettarello* in the upper part of Cori, the Temple of Hercules, where the place name *Giudaica* used for Piazza Orticara still survives today. At No. 25 in this square there is a building commonly held to have been the synagogue, and identifiable because of a low relief crest with a lily on the wall. There are no documents, however, to confirm this hypothesis.

Cori is a common surname for Roman Jews (→ Segni/Jewish surnames).

Farfa

Inhabitants 100
Altitude 138 m
Province of Rieti
Itinerary 3

This village grew up round the local abbey in the Middle Ages. It consists of a row of small houses of the same height with shops giving onto a road. These shops were rented by the monks to merchants who came in large numbers to Farfa for the April and September fairs. The completely abandoned village was restored by the last owner, Count Volpi di Misurata, at the beginning of this century. There is still a small monastic community living in the abbey.

A small group of Jews seems to have lived in the abbey area from 1402. From this date on, in fact, along with the other Jewish residents in the Lower Sabina and Rieti, the Farfa Jews had to send money to the Roman Jews who in turn had to pay a tax for the Agone and Testaccio games to the Camera Urbis. The Jews of the castle of Montopoli also depended on the abbot of Farfa. Among them were the Leuccio brothers, Elia and Iosef, who agreed on the sum to be paid as tax with the abbey.

The initial reason for the Jewish settlements in the small villages and castles in the Sabina area in the 14th and 15th century was the concession to open small loan-banks. But perhaps because of the very modest business mainly with farmers, the Jews soon threw themselves into all kinds of small rural enterprises, serving the Roman market and the traditional seasonal fairs in Sabina. In the 16th century there was a *contrada degli ebrei* ('Jewish quarter') in the fair area at Farfa, where the Jews were granted shops with a perpetual lease by the abbots.

Fondi

Inhabitants 18,000
Altitude 8 m
Province of Latina
Itinerary 2

Fondi, Piazza dell'Olmo Perino, known locally as the giudea

Fondi, Piazza dell'Olmo Perino, the building called the 'house of spirits'

Situated in the plain at the foot of the Aurunci hills, near the lake of the same name, the ancient settlement of *Fundi* was, according to legend, built by Hercules. The place name means 'property, farm'. Mainly a market town, Fondi provides local services for a fairly large population living scattered in the surrounding country-side.

Having developed along the Via Appia, the ancient centre still has the plan of a Roman encampment, with a *decumanus* and *cardo maximus*. Only one gate, the *Portella*, has survived of the original four gates to the town.

Our visit begins in Via Roma with the former church of *San Bartolomeo* (15th century), and continues along Viale Libertà. At the end of this street is a stretch of the town wall. One and a half kilometres long, the wall was built in the 3rd century BCE, but underwent considerable transformations in the Middle Ages. The overall layout, however, is still the same.

By taking Corso Appio Claudio you come to the Piazza della Repubblica with the 16th-century church of *Santa Maria Assunta*. It has a tripartite stone facade adorned in the central lunette by a fine Renaissance marble group. By continuing as far as the Piazza del Duomo, you can admire the medieval cathedral of *San Pietro* and the 16th-century *Palazzo del Principe*, whose facade overlooks Piazza Matteotti and Piazza dell'Unità d'Italia. In the latter square there is an isolated squared-based *Keep* tapering

up to a round top offering fine views, and the *Castle*, constructed from the 13th to the 15th century, but badly damaged during the Second World War. By going along Viale Vittorio Emanuele you come to Largo San Francesco and the 13th-century church of *San Francesco*, flanked by the building of the former *Monastery*, now the town hall. Inside the charming Gothic cloister there is a small local history museum. The war memorial in nearby Piazza De Gasperi has a mosaic panel by the sculptor Domenico Purificato (1972).

According to an extant document, there was once a Latin funeral inscription – now lost – from the Imperial age with an engraved *Menorah* (seven-branched candelabra) and the word 'Shalom' in Hebrew. This is the earliest trace of a Jewish presence in Fondi. A few centuries later Gregory the Great tells of a Jewish salesmen who, having stopped over for the night in the ruins of the temple of Apollo on the Via Appia, overheard demons plotting to send the Bishop of Fondi to hell. The attempt failed and the Jew was induced by Andrea himself to be converted.

In addition to these oral stories, documents testified to a Jewish presence in Fondi in 1280. The income from the *judaica*, the Jewish quarter, was given to the bishop and chapter of the cathedral by the Angevin sovereigns. Moreover, it was only natural that a town along the Via Appia, on the border between the Kingdom of Naples and the papal dominions, near the port of Terracina and Gaeta where Jews also lived, should become a place of residence for a community of traders and small-time craftsmen.

The living conditions of the Jews in Fondi were greatly improved with the rise of the Caetani family as local rulers. They took possession of the town in the late 13th century, making it the political and economic hub of their feudal possessions. They stimulated building activity through the construction of defensive works, churches, palaces and marshland reclamation. They also gave incentives to economic activities. Onorato II of Aragon, a Caetani, was one of the wealthiest and most powerful lords in the area. Under his rule, the Fondi Jewish community was particularly active in the textile trade, and almost had a total monopoly of the dyeing profession. In those years, a chapter in the town statutes expressly prohibited Jews (and anyone else exercising the profession of dyeing) from throwing dyed water into the public squares and streets. Significantly, the only rule hostile to Jews in the town statutes was that totally prohibiting them from selling ritually prepared meat to the Christians, even if the Christians themselves asked for it.

Relations between Jews and Christians in Fondi were thus good. The Jewish colony probably consisted of around 150 people, and in 1452-53, Alfonso V, King of Aragon and Sicily, exempted 'the Jews living in the lands of the Count of Fondi' from paying some taxes. In 1475 Ventura di Moyses from Fondi paid ten ducats to the bank of Filippo Strozzi as a deposit for the 1,050 ducats gifted for the wedding of Beatrice of Aragon from the Jews of Terra di Lavoro. In 1494, when the troops of Charles VIII, King of France, arrived in the region, many Jewish quarters were sacked. In 1495 Ventura di Moyses asked the Camera della Sommaria for permission to give up his moneylending activity to be allowed to go with his family and live in Gaeta. The following year the Fondi community began to dwindle, partly because of new restrictive measures and subsequent expulsions affecting Jews in southern Italy from 1510 to 1545.

In 1517 some representatives of the town of Fondi asked the Colonna, the new rulers of the town, if they could buy some houses and the synagogue belonging to the Jews, who had been 'absent from Fondi for a long time', thus marking the end of the long history of the Jewish settlements in the town.

Four centuries later, the memory of the ancient *giudea* has survived in popular tradition as the name for a group of now decaying medieval houses set round a court, situated between the town walls and Piazzetta dell'Olmo Perino. The small square is closed off by a building, which local legend has dubbed the 'house of spirits'. Recently, the position of the former synagogue has been traced to a nearby restored building at no. 9 Largo A. Rufo.

Frascati

Inhabitants 19,500
Altitude 320 m
Province of Rome
Itinerary 1

The place name Frascati derives either from the word *frasca*, a medieval permit enabling the inhabitants to cut firewood (*frasca* being the Italian for 'branch') in the local wood, or is simply a reference to the dense vegetation of the area. Situated at the edge of the Albani hills, this farming and commercial centre, renowned for its white wine, is the most famous of the Castelli Romani towns.

Our visit begins in Piazza Marconi, with its sweeping views as far as Rome. The square has a fine backdrop in the *Villa Aldobrandini*, while below are the grounds of the Villa Torlonia, now a municipal park. In the nearby Piazza San Pietro is the *Duomo*, built in the 16th and 17th century. The facade is by the sculptor Fontana (1700), who also designed the adjacent three-arched *Fountain*. Not far away is the 17th-century church of *Gesu*, while higher up is the medieval fort, later transformed into the *Palazzo Episcopale* (Bishop's Palace). Alongside is the Romanesque church of *Santa Maria in Vivario* (or *San Rocco*).

Frascati's principal attractions are its patrician villas: especially the 17th-century *Villa Aldobrandini* with its frescoed rooms and large grounds containing various fountains (it is the only villa open to the public), but also the *Villa Falconieri* and the *Villa Mondragone*.

At Frascati, in December 1326, Menachem Zemach, son of Avraham, probably of the Anaw family, the celebrated amanuenses whose codices are preserved in major Italian and foreign libraries, finished transcribing the *Book of Kings*, with comments by David Qimchi, Isaia da Trani and Beniamino, son of Guida Romano. Preserved in the Biblioteca Angelica, Rome, the parchment manuscript is part of the Oriental Codex no. 72. The text includes the 'Prophets' and 'Hagiographa', and its importance is due to the elaborate decorations and rare commentaries.

The presence of a Jewish group was documented in Frascati throughout the 16th century. The town is recorded in the register of localities paying the twentieth (1556), and in 1569 the synagogue made payments to the House of Catechumens. In 1728 the College of Cardinals ordered the Frascati bishops to prohibit Jews from living in the town without the prior authorisation of the congregation. Some Jews went back to live in Frascati at the turn of the 20th century. And in fact the oldest Jewish tombs in the municipal cemetery, just outside the town, date from this period.

Given the excellent vineyards in the area, Frascati kosher wine is produced in large quantities under the guidance of the Rome rabbinate.

Frascati became a Jewish surname (→ Segni/Jewish surnames).

In the late 15th century some Siena Jews opened a loan-bank in the nearby town of **Marino**, a strategic cross-roads for controlling communications between Rome and Naples. At the time the rulers of Marino, the Colonna family, who actually lived in the town, were at loggerheads with Pope Sistus v.

An earlier presence is documented, but the Jews already living in Marino were probably not moneylenders. This explains why the Colonna had to invite a Jewish family from Toscanella (→ Tuscania), who then moved to various towns, following a complicated route through Florence, Padua

and Rome. The head of this family was in contact with the leading members of Tuscan Jewry, and may have been a certain Isahac, who in 1472, although his wealth had been ascertained, refused to pay the special tax imposed on Jews by the papal Treasury.

Marino was also home to Elia di Leone (Eliahau ben Jehuda), physician and author of a Hebrew treatise on medicine, written in 1478, now in the Biblioteca Apostolica Vaticana.

Frosinone

Inhabitants 46,000
Altitude 291 m
Itinerary 2

Situated on top of a hill in the valley of the river Sacco, Frosinone is the centre of the Ciociaria, an area of Lazio embracing the Sacco (or Latina) Valley and the Ernici mountains. The earliest place name *Frusino* is of Volscian origin but its meaning is unclear.

No longer only a market town, today Frosinone is a fast-growing industrial centre and a road and rail junction linking Lazio and Campania. For this reason a modern residential area has grown up along the Via Casilina, not far from the A1 motorway exit, in the valley below the historic town centre.

Our visit to the historic centre begins in Piazza Vittorio Veneto with its panoramic views of the plain below and impressive palaces housing the Banca d'Italia and the Prefecture. After Piazza della Libertà, Via Plebiscito and Via Rattazzi, you come to the Romanesque cathedral of the *Assunta*, which was remodelled several times and completely rebuilt after the Second World War. Returning to Piazzale Vittorio Veneto, you take Corso della Repubblica with the Neoclassic church of *Santa Lucia*, and continue as far as Largo Turriziani, dominated by the Gothic entrance to the oldest part of the town. From here the long approach avenues wind back down to the plain.

The locality of *Fresolone*, better known as Frosinone, is recorded in three registers of taxes owed by Jews living in Campagna and Marittima. In all cases the tax was paid by the same person. Moreover, the reports on the implementation of the bull of Paul IV reveal that two of the investigated Jews were originally from Fondi and Ferentino and had only been living in Frosinone for a few months.

The lack of a group large enough to organise its own religious functions or even a wedding with Jews in nearby towns was among the main causes for the continuous moving of groups or single people from one locality to another.

There was no mention of a Jewish presence in Frosinone from the end of the 16th century until the mid 18th century, when several Jewish traders came back to stay for several months in the house of the priest Gaspari. The shops were probably re-opened at this time. From 1848 to 1853, making the most of an unexpected gesture of clemency from Pius IX, around forty Jews came to settle in Frosinone, including Angelo Sonnino, a Roman Jew granted an arms permit by the local police.

Not far away is **Monte San Giovanni Campano**. After the bull of Paul IV, many Jewish residents in the Papal States, rather than sell their property and be restricted in their commercial activities, chose to settle in this town, a feudal possession of Maria of Aragon, politically and administratively dependent on the governorship of Arpino in the Kingdom of Naples.

The resident Jews enjoyed special privileges and all the immunities granted by the local authorities. This attracted many Jews from the nearby community of **Pofi**, creating discontent in the local population, which decided to 'remove the privileged Jews'. But by petitioning Maria of Aragon, the permanently settled Jews obtained not only immunity for the newcomers but even more privileges. Maria of Aragon was again asked to intervene with the governor of Arpino after a number of Jews had been subject to inquisition by the Bishop of Veroli, for having exercised 'usury on usury'. Maria's intervention was to no avail, because the investigated Jews, Gabriele Sciabbadai and Issac were condemned in absentia and their property requisitioned. A further petition was made and this time, after the payment of twenty gold ducats, it was accepted by the Curia. Other Jews from Terracina and Pofi were brought to trial by the Apostolic Commissar, and they were all absolved, often after paying a fine.

From 1596 to 1598 three loan-banks were opened. They had five-year contracts, and one was run by a Jew from Terracina, Antonio, son of Giuseppe. A synagogue is also documented, since it paid ten scudi to the House of the Catechumens in Rome.

Gaeta

Inhabitants 25,000
Altitude 2 m
Province of Latina
Itinerary 2

Perched on the rocky Monte Orlando headland dividing the bay of Gaeta, the ancient settlement of *Caieta* took its name – according to the Virgilian tradition – from Aeneas' nurse. Others, however, claim it derives from the Greek for 'cavity' or 'cave'. Formerly a military stronghold, today it is a seaside resort, fishing port and oil terminal with various other industries.

The town is made up of several distinct parts. The medieval centre is at the tip of the promontory below Monte Orlando. The modern part of the town has grown up in the plain along the southern coast and round the harbours, while the seaside resort is strung out along the northern sandy beach of Serapo.

A good place to begin the visit to the medieval section, where there was a Jewish community until the 16th century, is the Lungomare Caboto. This seaside promenade goes past the *Roman Gates* and remains before arriving in Piazza Caboto, the headquarters of the port authorities. A number of streets branch off up from the waterfront: Via Annunziata with its *Monastery* and the 15th-century church of *Santissima Annunziata* with a Baroque facade, and Via Faustina which has the remains of a *Roman Villa*. Both streets wind sharply up the steep hill. From the same promenade you can reach the ancient cathedral of *Santi Erasmo e Marziano* (remodelled several times). Not far off are the remains of the *Ducal Palace of*

Docibele (10th century), providing access to the medieval quarter with its unspoilt allies, stairs and passageways.

After wandering through the medieval quarter, you can take Via Aragonese past the church of *San Domenico* (15th-century origins). The road goes on up to the *Castle*, consisting of two quadrilateral constructions, defended by towers, linked at various levels. The upper castle was built by the Aragonese and the lower castle by the Anjou. Having taken Via Angioina, you come to the 17th-century church of *Ulivi*, and immediately after the church of *San Francesco*, built in neo-Gothic style in the late 19th century. The road climbs up Monte Orlando to the *Mausoleum of Lucius Munazius Plancus*. Here there are fine views of the Gulf of Gaeta or – by taking a diversion before reaching the top – of the sanctuary of the *Santissima Trinità* (or *Montagna Spaccata*), set on a sheer drop down to the beach of Serapo.

As early as the Dark Ages there was a large Jewish community in the town. Their number then swelled when many Jews came from Spain in 1492, following the expulsion order by Ferdinand II the 'Catholic'. According to archive documents, their main activity was cloth dyeing and to exercise the profession they had to pay a special tax *pro utilitate civitatis*.

Gaeta's special geographical position on the Tyrrhenian coast meant it was an easy landing place for Jews coming from the Orient and bound for other Mediterranean cities. Thus, for example, in the mid 19th century Aharon ben Samuel ha-Nassi arrived from Baghdad. He was an expert on esoteric and mystical doctrines and had a large following.

The town statutes permitted and governed moneylending. In the 15th century the *Università* of Gaeta and its council asked Ferdinand, King of Naples, to expel a Jewish moneylender, because for every ounce of gold given as a loan, he demanded interest of 18 grains per month.

Genazzano

Inhabitants 4,800
Altitude 375 m
Province of Rome
Itinerary 1

This agricultural town stretched out over a hill has many medieval traces, mainly linked to the long period of feudal rule by the Colonna family.

The historic town is centred on Via Andreani, which begins at the crenellated town gate on Piazzale Matteotti and runs the length of the whole town, changing name several times before ending at the Colonna Castle. Along this long thoroughfare there are a number of interesting monuments: the small church of *Santa Croce* (15th century) dedicated to the war dead; the Romanesque church of *San Paolo* (remodelled in the 18th century); and the sanctuary of the *Madonna di Buon Consiglio* with an original Romanesque bell tower built in the 13th century, while the church itself was remodelled in Neoclassic style in the mid 19th century. The last stretch of the street, Corso Vannutelli, is lined by historic buildings some, such as the Gothic *Casa Apolloni* (said to be the birthplace of Oddone Colonna – Pope Martin V), and a nearby *15th-century House* are of special artistic interest. After the 16th-century shrine of the *Olio Santo*, the street ends at the *Colonna Castle*. Built in the Middle Ages, but later remodelled and extended, the castle maintains much of its original splendour.

The first evidence of a Jewish presence dates back to the 14th century, when a moneylender, a certain Sabatuccio, exercised his trade at

Genazzano, while among the residents were Elchanan, son of the physician Jehuda, and the physician Menachem, son of Jedidia. The community included a number of learned men, such as the amanuensis Jechiel da Genazzano, who in 1475 transcribed a manuscript (now in Oxford), and the poet and theologian Elia Chaim ben Benjamin, who wrote a work called *Iggheret Chamudot*, written to encourage David, the son of Rabbi Benjamin da Montalcino to study the Cabbala, and a poem dedicated to women.

Following the bull of Paul IV, the community sought refuge in a country place described as *Colle gentile* ('gentle hill'), where some people claim the remains of houses may still be seen today.

The Jewish presence is documented throughout the 16th century. Until 1569 there was a synagogue which paid 10 scudi to the House of the Catechumens. When the definitive expulsion of all Jews from the territories of the Papal States was decreed, the Genazzano community ended up in the Rome ghetto, where it joined the Scola Siciliana.

Montefiascone

Inhabitants 7,000
Altitude 590 m
Province of Viterbo
Itinerary 3

Set on a hill overlooking the lake of Bolsena, the ancient settlement was probably named after the site – a hill called *Mons Faliscorum*. A tourist resort, Montefiascone is renowned for its wines, such as the celebrated 'Est Est Est'. This unusual name – 'East East East' – is due to the enthusiastic cry made by the servant of a German notable, who is buried in the church of San Flaviano, sent to discover where to stop off and drink good wine.

Our visit to Montefiascone begins at the Romanesque church of *San Flaviano*. Remodelled in the 15th century, the interior has the unusual structure of two overlapping churches. From San Flaviano a street rises up as far as Piazza Roma, where the city gate (rebuilt in the 18th century) marks the entrance to the historic centre. By going along Corso Cavour as far as Piazza Vittorio Emanuele and past a large vault, you enter Largo Plebiscito with the Romanesque church of *Sant'Andrea*. From Via Filippini you reach Piazza Santa Monica and the *Duomo*. This majestic Renaissance construction was transformed at various times before the 19th century, when the Neoclassic portal was added to the facade. By taking Via Trento you come to a second town gate giving onto an open area with a fine view. The view becomes even more panoramic if, after going back through the gate, you take Via della Rocca and climb up as far as the top of the hill, where the remains of the old *Fort* stand.

In August the town has a local wine festival with a pageant and music, folk and sporting events.

The Jewish settlement in Montefiascone was encouraged by the town council, when to lift a siege by Orvieto it was forced to ask some Jewish bankers in Rome for a loan of 15,000 florins to pay the ransom demanded by the besiegers. As often happened, in exchange the bankers asked and obtained citizenship for themselves and their heirs, as well as full membership of the arts and crafts guilds. The Jews continued their moneylending activity in Montefiascone throughout the 15th century, and under Sistus V, who mitigated earlier papal bulls, they were granted further concessions. Giuseppe, son of Angelo di Viterbo thus had his licence renewed for five years. All that remains of this community today are a few Hebrew manuscripts (preserved in the local Biblioteca Vescovile) and a codex written in Perugia in 1391 by Jekuthiel, son of Immanuel, for Nethanel, son of Avraham di Montefiascone.

Bolsena, **Bagnoregio** and **Acquapendente**. Fifteen parchment manuscripts containing extracts of prayers, once in Bolsena are now in the Viterbo State Archives. They were certainly part of a single manuscript from the early 15th century. Many documents written from the 15th to 16th century have come from Bagnoregio and they testify to a Jewish presence that has long been neglected. The presence of individual Jews is documented along with a large community that enjoyed fairly favourable laws. The Bagnoregio Jews were allowed to close their commercial activities on Saturday and during Hebrew festivities. Moreover, they were granted equality in business with other citizens. Thus Amadio di Bonaventura di Castro, Vitale di Recanati and Benedetto Amadio were granted a licence for a loan-bank in 1546, while in 1553 another concession was given to Isach Benigno di Turano, a resident in Orvieto, in exchange for a loan of 200 gold scudi, after other members contacted by the town council had refused to lend the sum.

The town councils almost always encouraged Jewish settlements in their districts, because the Jews could provide them with the cash required to balance their books, almost always in the red because of the cost of continuous struggles to maintain or extend their territories. A town council register records the concession granted to the Jewish community for land to be used as a cemetery, situated near the field of San Francesco, near the vineyard of Nicola Pier Paolo. There are no other documents or evidence of this cemetery.

The Apostolic Chamber registers for the year 1326 record the presence of Jews who had arrived at Acquapendente from Rome. A number of 15th-century Hebrew manuscripts, mostly liturgical codices, came from this town. They were later used as covers for notarial registers. The lack of detailed information means that we are unable to locate the Jewish houses, although it is known for certain that the Jews lived in the town and had a synagogue. In 1591, with the consent of the Apostolic Chamber, a certain Pacifico 'Melvei' opened a loan-bank for three years.

It was easy to set up a moneylending activity in this safe and well-defended town. The Jews running the bank did not have to wear the badge and were granted citizenship. Thanks to these particularly favourable conditions, the whole Jewish group benefited indirectly from all those social and cultural services that were inevitably guaranteed wherever banks were opened.

In the early 20th century some Jewish families went back to live in Acquapendente. They continued, however, to be part of the Rome community. This new presence is documented by a letter of Auerlio Paggi and Elvira Servi written to inform the Community that although they lived in Acquapendente, they wished to continue to belong to the Pitigliano Community (which only ceased to exist in 1930), because their relatives were buried in the cemetery of the Tuscan town.

Orte

Inhabitants 7.820
Altitude 132 m
Province of Viterbo
Itinerary 3

Perched high on a tufa rock dominating a bend in the Tiber, the ancient Etruscan and Roman settlement of *Horte* probably owes its place name to the Latin for 'garden'. The town is now divided into two distinct parts: the medieval centre on the rock, and the modern part, an important rail junction on the Florence-Rome line, down in the plain.

The visit to medieval Orte begins from the Romanesque church of *San Silvestro*, at the entrance to the town. This church houses the *Museo Diocesano d'Arte Sacra* – a Museum of Sacred Art. From here Via Matteotti leads to the 18th-century *Palazzo Comunale*, whose interior includes frescoed rooms. Via Matteotti comes out in Piazza della Libertà with the 18th-century cathedral of the *Assunta*. Behind the cathedral is a maze of alleys, small squares and medieval passages. In the 16th century this was probably also the area of the Jewish settlement.

Yet again the first mention of Jews comes from archive documents. A number of mortgage and payment contracts drafted between Jews and Christians and some liturgical books, dated from the 13th to 14th century provide early information about the Jewish presence in the town, dating as far back as 1292. There must have been a fairly large community, since the town council had to take it into account when drafting the statute in 1584. Chapter Seven and Chapter

Twelve of the second book deal with the Jewish community. Chapter Seven establishes that Jews could not be solicitors in civil law suits, while Chapter Twelve defined the duration of loans. Chapter Thirty-Six of Book v, although dealing with other laws, indirectly proves the existence of a cemetery, or rather Jewish graves, in a place called 'Misciano', outside the city walls. This zone was probably a farm called 'Miciano', but no trace of gravestones has ever been found there. After the bull of Paul IV, the Orte Jews were probably concentrated in Contrada Porcini, the area bounded by the present-day Via Don Minzoni, Via Frattini and Piazza Montecavallo.

At the end of the 19th century there was a Via del Ghetto, now Via Poerio in the Contrada San Sebastiano. Not far away, at no. 25 Via Milazzo, a 13th-century building is known in the town as the House of Columns or *Casa di Juda* ('House of Judas'). The second name, according to the townspeople, does not refer to a possible owner, but to the fact that in the Middle Ages the owner of the house had betrayed his own faction.

Ronciglione and **Soriano nel Cimino.** In the Ronciglione town statute books there are various sections dealing with Jews living in the town. Today, perhaps to perpetuate the memory of the old original Jewish quarter, a cul-de-sac is still called *Vicolo del Ghetto*.

There are ten extant parchment manuscripts, formerly in a 15th-century biblical codex, from Soriano nel Cimino. On 26 October 1867, a shopkeeper, Sabatino Panzieri from Rome, applauded the arrival of Garibaldi's troops in the town. It seems that Sabatino also made a tricolour Italian flag and some shirts for the liberators.

There were also small groups of Jews at **Nepi**, where Jechiel Manoscrivi circumcised Binjamin, son of David, and at **Capranica**, where there were eleven 15th-century biblical manuscripts, later used as covers for notarial registers; the manuscripts are now in the Viterbo State Archives.

Ronciglione, an alley in the ghetto

Ostia

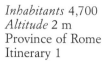

Inhabitants 4,700
Altitude 2 m
Province of Rome
Itinerary 1

In ancient times Ostia grew from a farming village at the mouth of the Tiber to be the main port of Rome, and now is a very interesting archaeological zone. Our visit begins with the *Castle*, and the *Museo della Rocca* next door, before proceeding inside the *Ancient Ostia* excavation zone. Following the main street to the ancient city, we find the principal Roman monuments, such as the baths, theatre, temples and forum. The *Synagogue* is in an isolated position at the end of the main street – the *decumanus*.

Ostia was a busy trading centre and this explains the presence of various foreign groups in the town. There are no archive documents about Jews in Ostia, but the discovery of a synagogue in 1961 during works on the road to the Fiumicino airport provides impressive evidence of their presence. Situated near the former coastline, along the Via Severiana (built over a previous road layout), the synagogue is reached by going along the main street (*decumanus*) as far as Porta Marina, and then turning left to follow a north-east direction. The temple was probably built in the second half of the 1st century CE. It was modified and enlarged in the following two centuries, before being radically re-modelled sometime between the end of the 3rd and the beginning of the 4th century.

The synagogue consists of a series of rooms arranged in an east-west direction on an area of 23.5 x 36.6

Ostia synagogue, detail of mosaic paving

*Ostia synagogue, front of the
monumental niche*

Ostia synagogue, rear of the monumental niche

metres. The main rectangular worship room (approx. 25 x 12.5 meters) is reached by going through a narthex – a porticoed vestibule, given a monumental feel by four columns. The furthest curving wall was fitted with a *tevah*. On the opposite side, there is a niche – probably for the *aron* – preceded by two small columns with corbels (now cast copies) supporting the horizontal beams, decorated with a *menorah* and flanked by a *shofar* and a *lulav*. The vestibule also leads into a room, which at some point was transformed into a kitchen with an oven (possibly for baking unleavened bread) and recipients (*dolia*) for food. Beyond this room is another space – again from the late period of the temple – with large benches along the walls. It may have been the guest room. Lastly, there was a cistern beneath the vestibule.

In addition to the traditional synagogue corbels, the museum also contains some lamps with *menorah*s from the synagogue. But the most interesting item is an inscription. Found on a tablet in the synagogue, after dedication to the health of the sovereign in Latin, the inscription continues with a self-celebratory passage in Greek by Mindis Faustos who had gifted the *aron*. In fact this man borrowed the first six lines of an existing text (perhaps referring to other parts of the synagogue) and adapted it to suit his own case, using only the last line, while the others were deliberately rubbed out.

The Pianabella necropolis is closely connected to Ostia. It has yielded an interesting epitaph dedicated to Plotius Fortunatus, the archsynagogue, on a plaque raised by his children and wife. Together with a gravestone now in the Roman National Museum (→ Rome/Itinerary VIII), these are the only epigraphs concerning the Ostia Jewish community.

Lastly, some epitaphs found in a graveyard in Via Laurentina, known to be used by the inhabitants of Ostia, have typically Semitic names (Apelle, Achiba and Aciba).

Detail of the shelf in front of the aron

Further down the coast is the town of **Nettuno**. Archive documents from the late 15th century mention the Jews Gratiano and Salomone, who paid 5 and 10 baiocchi for twentieths and 20 baiocchi in interest. In the 16th century there was a synagogue in Nettuno, which paid 10 scudi to the House of the Catechumens in Rome. The whereabouts of the synagogue is not known.

Palestrina

Inhabitants 13,500
Altitude 450 m
Province of Rome
Itinerary 1

Nestling on the slopes of Monte Ginestro, the ancient town of *Praeneste* was probably named after the site of the earliest settlement. Today the town is set on terraces with parallel streets at different heights linked by steep stairs cutting vertically into the slope of the hill. There are many archaeological remains and medieval monuments, either in various historical layers or still standing side by side.

Starting from Via della Stazione, we go through the *Porta del Sole* (with the crest of the Barberini family) to Piazzale Santa Maria degli Angeli, which includes stretches of the *Megalithic Walls*, and up Via Anicia (also with wall remains), as far as the central square, Piazza Regina Margherita with the cathedral of *Sant'Agapito*. Originally built by the Romans with tufa, the church was transformed in the Middle Ages and then enlarged in later centuries. Consisting of a nave and two aisles separated by pillars, the interior contains several interesting paintings, frescoes, ancient inscriptions and statues. Along the side of the *Duomo* are ancient Roman remains, while the backdrop to the square is the massive building of the former *Seminary*. Two rooms in this building – the Sala Absidata and the Antro delle Sorti – incorporate pre-Roman remains.

Having left the square, you climb up as far as Piazza della Cortina with the monumental *Sanctuary* (2nd-1st century BCE) below the *Palazzo Colonna Barberini.* Rebuilt in its present form in 1640, this palace houses a local archaeology museum – the *Museo Nazionale Archeologico Prenestino*. By leaving the square from Via Barberini, you reach the church of *San Francesco*, rebuilt in the 15th century. Part of the local Jewish community lived round this church. After winding up Via del Tempio, you come to the town hall, the Porta San Martino, and the church of *San Martino* with the nearby *Bishop's Palace*.

Palestrina is the birthplace of Giovanni Pierluigi da Palestrina (1525-94), an early composer of polyphonic music.

In 1472 four Jewish households were recorded as having paid a total of 15 ducats to Iacobus de Aquasparta, the collector of twentieths, from Jews living in Campagna and Marittima. Archive and bibliographical sources help us in more or less identifying where these houses were located. A late 15th-century cadastre indicates that the quarters of San Francesco and Portella had many cellars, stables and houses given *alli Giudi* ('to the Jews'). The cadastre also indirectly attests to the existence of a synagogue in a house in the Portella quarter. An 18th-century historian provides further information, claiming that in his day the village of Palestrina was disdainfully referred to as 'vile, because in 1562, Jews lived there and they must have had their synagogue in Via del Borgo'. The areas and streets mentioned still exist and are in the town centre.

Tax registers record a Jewish presence in many towns along the Via Prenestina, an important road since Roman days: **Zagarolo**, **Cave**, **Gallicano nel Lazio**, **Paliano**, **Piglio** and **Valmontone**. As many as 13 Jewish households paid taxes in the town of Valmontone. Official statistics for the year 1853 reveal that in Zagarolo there were four male Jews out of a population of 4,430.

Priverno

Inhabitants 13,000
Altitude 151 m
Province of Latina
Itinerary 2

Situated on a hillock in the valley of the Amaseno, until 1928 this town was called Piperno, from the Latin *pipernus*, meaning a black spongy volcanic stone. In 1928 it resorted back to an Italian version of its original Volscian name *Privernum*, after Priverio, the supposed founder of the town. Today Priverno is an important agricultural centre with a food industry.

The historic centre dates back to the Middle Ages, while the Volscian and Roman zone are outside the town. The modern expansion has mainly taken place along the plain.

By beginning our tour in Piazza xx Settembre and going through the Romanesque town gate, you come to the 15th-century church of *Sant'Antonio Abate*. Leaving the square by Via Consolare, with the Gothic church of *San Nicolò* (remodelled in the 18th century) you proceed along Via Zaccaria as far as Porta San Marco and the church of the *Suffragio*, to come out in the main square, Piazza Vittorio Emanuele II. This square has a number of interesting buildings: the Gothic cathedral of *Maria Assunta*, the monumental *Palazzo Comunale* (town hall), also Gothic, and the 15th-century *Palazzo Seneca*. By going back up Via Felice Orsini from Via Consolare you pass picturesque houses with external stairs and the church of *San Giovanni Evangelista* and the remains of its Gothic bell tower. Via Consolare also leads to Porta Napoletana, and the descent down to Piazzale San Benedetto, the oldest part of the town with the church of *San Benedetto* (9th century) and the former *Palazzo Comunale.*

The earliest mention of Jews is found in a notarial deed recording, in the presence of the Bishop of Terracina, the conversion of a young Jewish woman, subsequently adopted by the canon of the church of Santa Maria di Sermoneta. Another early document records a protest made by the Jew Salomone, who had been considered a *habitator urbis* rather than a citizen of Priverno for the purposes of a tax levied by Paul II on Jews required to contribute to the games of Agone and Testaccio. As a consequence Salomone had to pay a higher figure than other Jews living outside Rome.

Although the town statutes included the usual heavy restrictions, they also included a clause banning Christians from summoning Jews to civil court cases on Hebrew feast days. Both Books I and V reiterated the necessity for Jews to supply the *bravia* – banners to be paraded during the *palio* and feast days of the local patron saints.

After returning to Priverno in the 20th century to open a fabrics shop, the Sonnino family continued this tradition by providing the cloths for the *palio* at their own expense. The family went to live in the Cancello area where Jews had also lived after the bull of Paul IV.

Having been enclosed in the ghetto of Rome after their definitive expulsion from the Papal States, the Priverno Jews were members of the Scola Tempio (→ Rome, Itinerary I) and many of them then went to Leghorn, where they were favourably received.

Priverno was the birthplace of the rabbi and intellectual Avraham Barukh (1863), son of Moshe Rafael Piperno, the author of an anthology of Hebrew verse entitled *Qol Uggav.* According to Ministry of Trade fig-ures there was a new Jewish presence in Priverno in the 19th century: 7 inhabitants practised the Jewish religion out of a total population of 4,873.

Piperno is now a common Roman Jewish surname (→ Segni/Jewish surnames).

THE JEWS FROM SOUTHERN ITALY
The introduction in Sicily of the expulsion measures (1492) by the Spanish sovereigns Ferdinand and Isabella brusquely ended the long history of Jewish settlements on the island. In as little as around fifty years, the Jews in the Kingdom of Naples also had to take the way of exile, and soon there were no more Jews in southern Italy, except for baptised Jews, who covertly continued the faith of their fathers. They have only been identified by recent historical research.

The southern Italian Jews gradually drifted northwards, stopping first in Naples, Catanzaro and Reggio Calabria. But as the situation grew tenser, they began to arrive in the towns on the border between Lazio and Campania, while their ultimate destination was to be Rome.

From the end of the 15th century to the early 16th century, there were Jews from Sicily and the Kingdom of Naples in Cori, Sermoneta, Sezze and Priverno.

The towns in the regions once called Campagna and Marittima (now southern Lazio) offered the nearest initial refuge. Here the southern Italian Jews established relations of work, friendship and family. And as was documented in the 1630s and 1640s, marriages were celebrated and hereditary deals struck. In the cover for a notarial protocol for the years 1561-70 (now in the Latina State Archives) there was a parchment fragment containing the rare text of liturgical verse for the festivities of *Sukkoth*, probably of Sicilian origin. In the second half of the century, when Jews were definitively expelled from the Kingdom of Naples and forced to live in Rome, the Jews in

Campagna and Marittima, including the southern Italian and Sicilian refugees, went to join their Roman relatives who had directly sought asylum in Rome immediately after their expulsion.

In **Sonnino,** not far from Priverno, only one Jew is recorded as having paid the twentieth in the 15th century. This does not imply, however, that there was only one Jew or even one Jewish household in the town. In other towns the tax was often played by only one person for the whole local community.

Sonnino is one of the most common Roman Jewish surnames (→ Segni/Jewish surnames).

Rieti

Inhabitants 43,500
Altitude 405 m
Itinerary 3

Situated on the river Velino at the feet of Monte Terminillo, the ancient town of *Reate* was of Sabine origin. Today a provincial capital, it is a lively agricultural and industrial town, and the chief market town for the whole of the Rieti basin.

The historic centre still has its original Roman layout: the main square Piazza Vittorio Emanuele II (on the ancient forum) is the crossroads for the *cardo* (Via Roma and Via Pennina) and the *decumanus* (Via Garibaldi and Via Cintia). The main architectural and artistic heritage is concentrated in this area, while the modern town has sprung up all round.

Our visit begins in Piazza Vittorio Emanuele II with the 15th-century *Palazzo Comunale* (remodelled several times), which houses the town museum (archaeology, painting and sculpture collections), a public library and the civic archives. In nearby Piazza Battisti is the *Palazzo del Governo*, formerly the Palazzo Poiani, named after the lords of Piediluco – its Italian style garden offers fine views. This is also the area of the cathedral of the *Assunta*: a medieval basilica completely remodelled in the 17th century with a Romanesque bell tower. The cathedral treasury is housed in the baptistery. In the middle of nearby Piazza Vittori is a monument to *St Francis* by sculptor Giovanni Nicoletti (1926) flanked by the 13th-century *Palazzo Vescovile* (Bishop's Palace) and a loggia supported by two broad arcades. Having gone past the *Bishop's Arch*, built at the behest of Boniface VIII, at the foot of the Palazzo Vescovile in Via dell'Episcopio is the 15th-century church of *San Pietro Martire*, whose 17th-century interior is particularly grandiose.

We then go along Via Cintia, lined with impressive Renaissance palaces including the *Palazzo Vincentini*, attributed to Antonio da Sangallo il Giovane (1483-1546). About halfway along this street, in the adjacent Piazza della Beata Colomba, is the church of *San Domenico*. Built in the 15th century, it was remodelled in the 17th century, while the cloister was added in the 19th century. Coming back along Via Cintia, you pass Piazza Marconi, with views of the perfectly preserved 13th-century walls built along the same line as the earlier Roman walls. Having gone along Viale Ludovio Canali as far as Piazza Mazzini and the station, you can visit the Gothic church of *Sant'Agostino*, radically restructured inside during the 19th century. After going through the gardens of Piazza Oberdan, bounded by noble palaces (Palazzo Ricci and the Palazzo Podestà, later incorporated in the Palace of the Seminary), you take Via della Pescheria. From the 15th to 16th century the local Jewish group was concentrated in this area. From here, by going along Via Centurioni, you come to the *Teatro Flavio Vespasiano*, a theatre opened in 1893 whose entrance gives onto Via Garibaldi.

The longest street in Rieti, running the whole length of the historic centre from east to west, partly following the route of the ancient Via Salaria, Via Garibaldi has a number of impressive palaces.

From Piazza Vittorio Emanuele II you enter Via Roma. In addition to various 15th-century buildings, at the end of this busy shopping street is the 14th-century church of *San Francesco*, completely remodelled in the 18th century; inside is a cycle of frescoes by the school of Giotto.

Halfway along Via Roma you turn into Via Pelliceria to visit the Romanesque church of *San Pietro* and the grandiose Renaissance *Palazzo Vecchiarelli*, with its stage-like courtyard. This street ends at the bridge over the Velino. Alongside are the remains of a 1st-century Roman bridge offering a fine panoramic view. Outside the town is the *Roman Gate* at the junction with the Via Salaria.

In 1342 the constitutional rules for the diocese of Sabina were promulgated. They included a number of restrictions for Jews established by canon law reiterated for Jews living in the diocese. This is the first indirect evidence (along with the transcription of a Hebrew manuscript in Rieti in 1311) of a Jewish presence in this area as early as the first half of the 14th century.

In 1344 a manuscript was written in Rieti, now in the town archives, with a Hebrew signature. But there was no more mention of Jews in Rieti until the end of the century. From 1408 the town reforms regularly included chapters dedicated to Jewish moneylenders from Rome. They supplied the town with money to pay the military commanders serving the commune, involved in continuous fighting with neighbouring Terni and Cittaducale, as well as internecine struggles.

The Rieti Jews were not only moneylenders, however. They also included illustrious physicians and rabbis, such as Mose di Isac da Rieti and Emanuele di Terni, *expertissimus in fisica et cirorgia* who served the commune in 1478, and traders, especially in foodstuffs, such as cheese, oil and sugar.

MOSE DA RIETI

Born in Rieti in 1388, Mose was the son of Isac (or Gaio). This renowned physician soon moved to Rome, where in 1422 he became archiater to Paul Pius II. He always kept in touch, however, with his native town, where his family ran a loan-bank and a number of commercial enterprises.

Mose was also a poet and philosopher. Among his written works is a Hebrew book of verse *Miqdas Me'at* ('The little sanctuary'), inspired by Dante's *Divine Comedy,* and a philosophical treatise, *Filosofia naturale e fatti de Dio*, written in Italian with some local dialect influences and Hebrew letters. The Roman Jews appointed him to collect the contributions from the other Jewish communities to pay the taxes to the Apostolic Chamber.

From 1422 to the second half of the century, the names of Dattolo and Ventura di Angelo often appear alongside that of Moses.

The Rieti Jews had a relatively quiet life. In the Archivio Capitolare there is a Brief by Paul II to the priest serving the Bishop of Rieti, threatening excommunication for all those who had unjustly confiscated the goods of the Jews Samuele and Mose di Angelo di Dattilo, if they failed to return them. From 1466, however, the Rieti Jews had to wear the badge (a large yellow round form for men and ring shaped earrings, called *circelli* for women). They were also subject to other restrictions, such as the ban on employing Christian wet nurses. There is a rather interesting law prohibiting Christians from lighting fires, carrying wood or doing any other service for Jews on the Sabbath, when the Jews were supposed to abstain from any kind of work.

The Christians could not buy unleavened bread and other food prepared by Jews, who could, however, 'sell, exchange' pickled tuna, fish, domestic and wild bees, and other animals (provided they were not slaughtered ritually), vegetables, fruit and wheat.

In 1444 Bernardino da Feltre preached against the Jews at Rieti, probably paving the way to restrictive laws introduced two years later. In 1489 the Franciscans established the *Monte di Pietà* and the *Monte Frumentario* ('wheat bank') at an interval of a few months in a deliberate attempt to win over the trade in money and grain from the Jews. Thus the Jews' physical, economic and social space in the town gradually dwindled until their definitive expulsion in 1569. Previously the Jews had lived freely in all the quarters of the town, although they tended to concentrate in the area called 'Porta Carceraria di Dentro'. In 1509, however, they were confined to only one street, where they were assigned a number of houses, going from the Palazzo dei Priori to the Palazzo del Podestà – what is today Via della Peschiera.

In the neighbouring valleys, the Jewish presence was often only a single household owning a loan-bank. They lived at **Aspra** (known since 1947 as **Casperia**) where the town statutes of 1397 refer to Jewish moneylenders, as well as at **Torano**, **Montopoli**, **Magliano**, **Nerola**, **Palombara**, **Monterotondo** and **Fara**, where Jewish households paid the special 'twentieth' tax.

On the road from Rieti to Rome, at **Cantalupo Sabino**, a Hebrew epigraph was found, written to the memory of Palomba Baraffael, who died at a young age in 1813. Since at that time the measures introduced by Urban VIII against placing gravestones and the order to remove them were in force, the family may have taken this gravestone from the Aventine cemetery with them when they settled in Rieti. The Baraffael family, originally from Ancona, and had been one of the wealthiest and most important families living in the Roman ghetto, where they were spice merchants and members of the Scola Nova (→ Rome/Itinerary I).

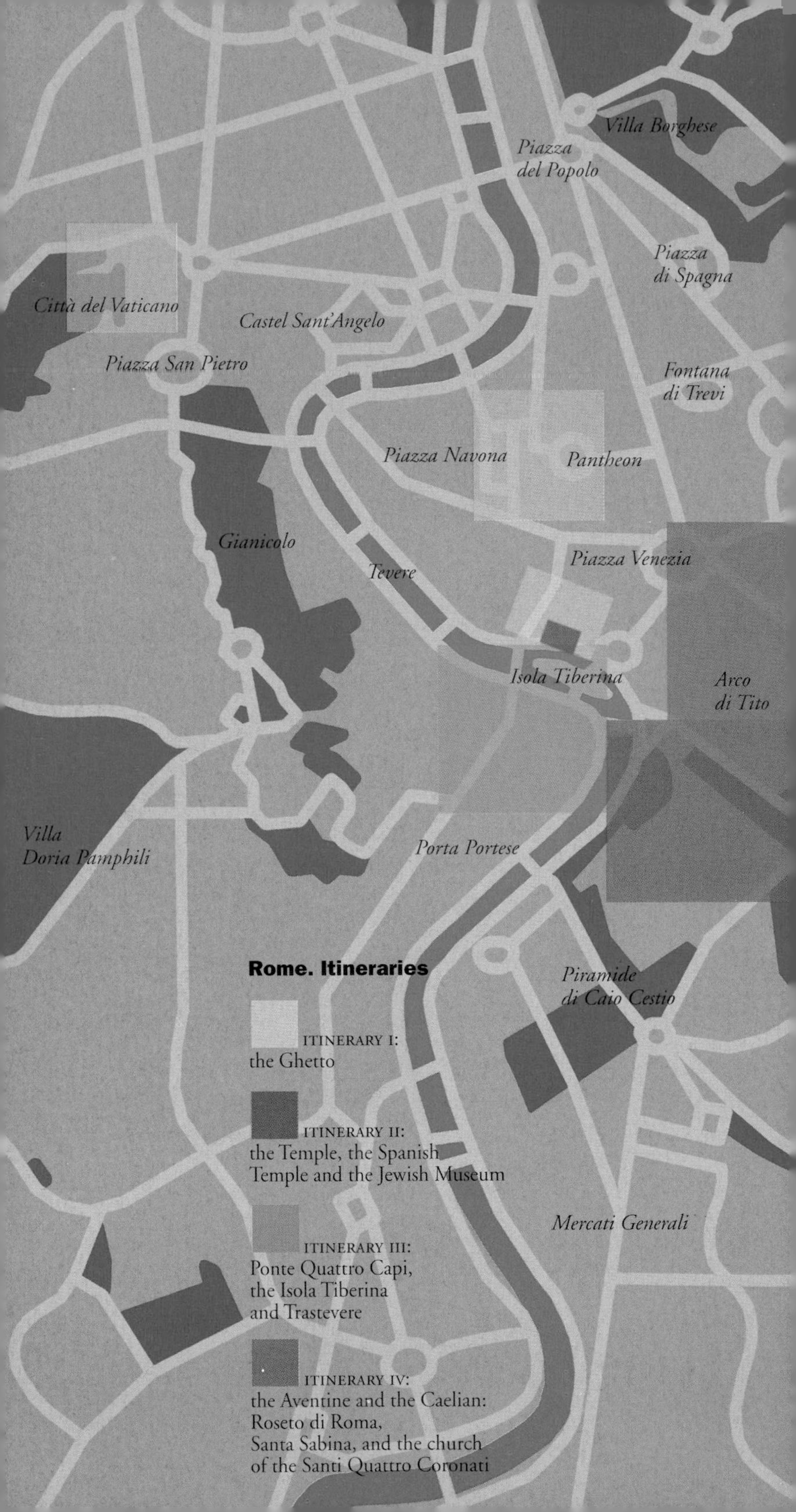

Villa Borghese

Piazza
del Popolo

Piazza
di Spagna

Città del Vaticano

Castel Sant'Angelo

Piazza San Pietro

Fontana
di Trevi

Piazza Navona

Pantheon

Gianicolo

Piazza Venezia

Tevere

Isola Tiberina

Arco
di Tito

Villa
Doria Pamphili

Porta Portese

Piramide
di Caio Cestio

Rome. Itineraries

ITINERARY I:
the Ghetto

ITINERARY II:
the Temple, the Spanish
Temple and the Jewish Museum

ITINERARY III:
Ponte Quattro Capi,
the Isola Tiberina
and Trastevere

Mercati Generali

ITINERARY IV:
the Aventine and the Caelian:
Roseto di Roma,
Santa Sabina, and the church
of the Santi Quattro Coronati

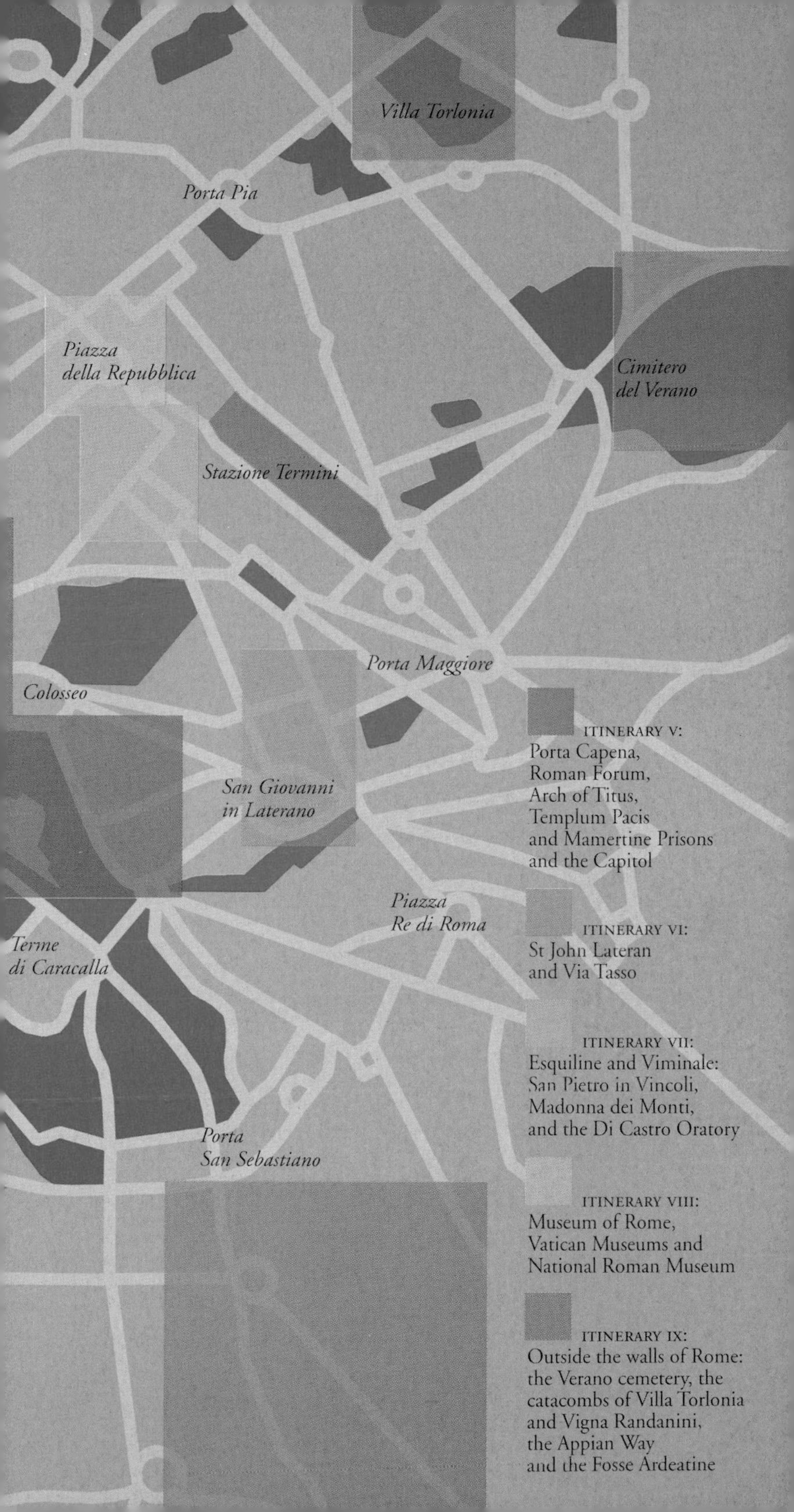

Villa Torlonia

Porta Pia

Piazza
della Repubblica

Cimitero
del Verano

Stazione Termini

Porta Maggiore

Colosseo

San Giovanni
in Laterano

ITINERARY V:
Porta Capena,
Roman Forum,
Arch of Titus,
Templum Pacis
and Mamertine Prisons
and the Capitol

Piazza
Re di Roma

ITINERARY VI:
St John Lateran
and Via Tasso

Terme
di Caracalla

ITINERARY VII:
Esquiline and Viminale:
San Pietro in Vincoli,
Madonna dei Monti,
and the Di Castro Oratory

ITINERARY VIII:
Museum of Rome,
Vatican Museums and
National Roman Museum

Porta
San Sebastiano

ITINERARY IX:
Outside the walls of Rome:
the Verano cemetery, the
catacombs of Villa Torlonia
and Vigna Randanini,
the Appian Way
and the Fosse Ardeatine

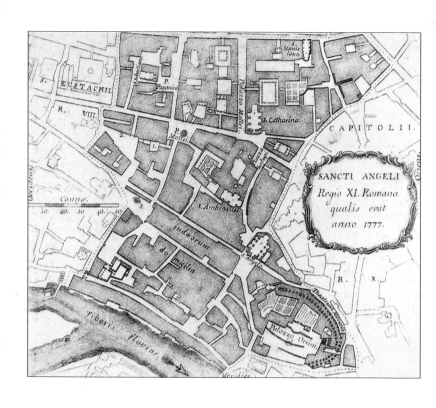

Map of the Sant'Angelo district, 1777;
the ghetto is indicated with the words
judaeorum domicili

Rome

Population: 2,900,000
Altitude: 20 m

The centre of Italy's cultural and political life, Rome has one of the greatest concentrations of artistic treasures and historic monuments in the world. For a complete description of these treasures, see a general guide to the city; the present guide is only concerned with the monuments and artistic records that trace the two-thousand-year history of the Jewish community – from the Rome of the emperors through the Rome of the popes to the Rome of the modern Italian Republic. The places of interest have been divided into nine different itineraries.

Itinerary ɪ: the Ghetto

The age-old presence of a Jewish community in the city is commonly identified with one specific area – that bounded by the Isola Tiberina section of the Tiber, the Ponte Fabricio (Ponte Quattro Capi), Via del Portico d'Ottavia (as far as the monument giving the street its name) and Piazza delle Cinque Scole. This is hardly surprising since Jews were already living here in Roman times. In the 13th century the community gradually shifted away from Trastevere to settle in even larger numbers in this area.

This was the area designated by Pope Paul ɪv in the bull of 14 July 1555 as Rome's ghetto. That edict initiated three centuries of physical confinement and moral subjugation within what became known as the 'Jew's enclosure'. And even today, when Jews live freely throughout the city, the ghetto or 'the piazza' – as the Jewish quarter is familiarly known – is a point of reference for the community's cultural and emotional life. The ghetto is the place of personal and collective memories for Roman Jews. They gather here for both celebration and commemoration, to pass evenings together or to observe religious holidays. Rich in traces of Rome's long past, the area's charm and atmosphere is appreciated by Romans and visitors alike. Situated between the foot of the Capitol and the banks of the Tiber, the area had an important strategic position, evidenced by a number of imposing Classical monuments: the Portico of Octavia, the Theatre of Marcellus and the Flaminian Circus. In the Middle Ages the economic and political importance of the area continued to grow as a number of powerful noble families encouraged the growth of crafts and trade. But then came the over-crowding and over-building during confinement, only brought to an end when the entire zone was demolished in the late 19th century. Thereafter the area was given an entirely new urban layout, the key building being the new Temple, built in 1904.

From an archaeological, historical and urban point of view the area has many layers of history, and the itinerary has been drawn up in such a way that the visitor gets some idea of the events and the life in the Jewish community in relation to the district as a whole. Given that any itinerary naturally involves some chronological 'leaps', for an overall account of the history of the Jewish community in Rome, see the historical notes in the Introduction.

Our visit begins at the junction of Via Catalana and Via del Tempio, just beyond the gates to the synagogue. From this point there is a good view of the area once occupied by the ghetto. Divided by the cross-roads, this site now forms four urban blocks containing

*The Portico of Ottavia at the
end of the 19th century
(Archivio fotografico comunale)*

The Portico of Ottavia at night

the Temple and its surrounding garden, two apartment blocks built at the time of Umberto I, two schools (Ugo Foscolo and Quintino Sella, on Via del Portico d'Ottavia), and four small Art-Nouveau-style villas in the area between Lungotevere Cenci, Via Catalana, Via del Tempio and Piazza delle Cinque Scole. The ghetto was razed during the period 1886-1904, in line with the 1873 urban plan to make Rome a fitting capital for the new kingdom of Italy. The city council implemented this radical 'slum clearance' scheme by applying legislation passed to deal with the most unhealthy and run-down areas of Naples. Documents show that the Jewish community 'accepted with resignation, taking into due consideration the need for architectural propriety in Rome'. The Roman Jews were, in fact, anxious to put an end to more than three centuries of confinement in an area that had become practically uninhabitable, and they marked the end of this grim chapter in their history by the construction of a large temple for the entire community. The building was to be a landmark in the new urban layout of Rome, a symbol of emancipation and re-acquired freedom.

In line with the criteria applied in those days, demolition was total and indiscriminate – concerned simply with clearing the area to make way for the transformation and renovation of the new capital. Dangerous buildings and unhealthy alleyways were razed, but so also were buildings of great historical and artistic interest, such as the Cinque Scole. The only surviving parts of the old synagogues are the precious furnishings now in the Temple and in the Di Castro Oratory in Via Balbo (→ Itinerary VII).

Via del Portico d'Ottavia, Via Della Reginella and Piazza delle Cinque Scole still contain many traces of what ghetto life must have been like; and you can get some idea of the actual urban fabric by looking at nearby buildings not demolished during the ghetto clearance. An interesting comparison can be drawn between a present-day map of the area and the Gregorian Cadastre of 1816: present-day buildings are outlined in red, while underneath in black you can see the tight network of streets and alleyways forming the ghetto. The ghetto covered some 30,000 square metres (including 23,000 square metres of housing). But while the population affected by the original decree of 1555 totalled 1,750 people, by the time emancipation came some 5,000 people lived in the ghetto and the area had one of the highest population densities in Rome. This explains why houses continually expanded in the only direction open to them – upwards. Wood and metal structures were added to make extra floors on top of the original buildings, thus precariously raised to six or seven storeys. The limit of the 'Jew's Enclosure' stretched approximately the length of the present day Via Catalana and Largo del Tevere (without the embankment), reaching about two-thirds of the way up the present-day Via del Portico d'Ottavia. The front of the medieval and Renaissance buildings in this street up to Piazza Cotaguti thus lay outside the ghetto.

Walking down Via Catalana alongside the Temple garden you come to the square in front of the monumental propylaea of the *Portico of Octavia*. The building was started by Q. Cecilius Metellus in 146 BCE, that is, around the same time that the first Jews were settling in Rome in this very area. It has since become something of a symbol for the Jewish quarter as a whole, a silent witness to the whole history of the community in Rome – from the original settlement, through the establishment of the ghetto to the house-to-house raids carried out by the Nazis in 1943. Originally called the *Porticus Metelli*, it enclosed temples dedicated to Jupiter Stator and Juno the Queen (two large columns with Corinthian capitals from the second temple now form part of the building at no. 5 Via Sant'Angelo in Pescheria, and are partially visible

Buildings from various periods side by side in Via del Portico d'Ottavia

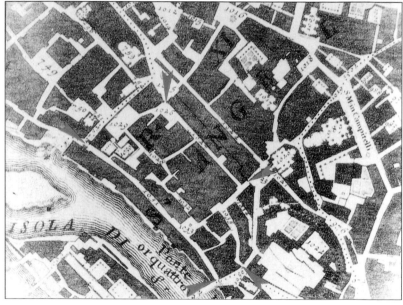

Via di Pescaria, now Via del Portico d'Ottavia, 1887 (Archivio fotografico comunale)

The ghetto in G. B. Nolli's map of Rome, clearly showing the five gates, 1748

Piazzetta del Pancotto, 1886
(Archivio fotografico comunale)

from the buildings opposite). The Portico was entirely re-built and extended in 27-23 BCE under Augustus, who dedicated it to his sister Octavia. Adorned with fine statues by Phidias, Praxiteles and Lysippus, the structure housed a Greek and a Latin library and extended in a covered double colonnade to the present-day Piazza Campitelli. All that remains of this vast centre of classical learning is one of the two propylaeum. The inscription refers to rebuilding carried out at the time of Septimus Severus and Caracalla (203 CE) after it had been badly damaged by two fires. To the right of the Portico of Octavia you get a fine view of the archaeological site with the Theatre of Marcellus (begun under Caesar and completed under Augustus, who dedicated it to his dead nephew in 23 BCE) and the temples of Apollo Soranus and Bellona.

Amidst these imposing remnants of Classical Rome, there was – from the 10th century onwards – a steady increase in the trade and crafts that had originally attracted the Jews to the area. These building stood at the end of the *Via Peregrinorum*, a main thoroughfare in medieval Rome. The arches of the Theatre of Marcellus housed butchers, lime kilns, carpenter's shops, tanning works, cloth and silk vendors and the stalls of some of Rome's first money-changers (*campsores*). Under the barrel vaults of the Portico of Octavia, on the other hand, marble blocks recovered from the Classical ruins were used as slabs for a fish market – hence the medieval name of Via di Pescaria (the present day Via del Portico d'Ottavia). The front of the building still bears a marble inscription banning gambling and another plaque recording that the 'Conservators of Rome' had the right to the head of any fish more than five spans in length. Another inscription (1581) reiterating this right includes a marble outline of a fish and the way the head is to be measured (*usque ad primas pinnas*). It is now on the wall of the entrance staircase to the Capitoline Museum in the Palazzo dei Conservatori (→ Itinerary v). Roman Jews still recount that, after passing from hand to hand, the fish concerned reached the august personage of the Conservator in a rather less than perfect state.

The legend of the Jewish pope is closely linked with the Theatre of Marcellus area, where the Pierleoni family lived. Like the Crescenzi, the De Cintiis and the Savelli, they were one of the noble families that offered their protection to craftsmen and tradesmen – and thus to the Jews – in the area. One of the most virulent arguments used in the bitter controversy surrounding Pierleoni, the antipope Anacletus II (1130-38), concerned his supposedly Jewish origins. His family, it was claimed, descended from a certain Barukh or Benedetto, a converted Jew. Whether true or not, the story does reveal the close links between the Jews and the powerful families who lived in this area and left traces in such place names as Lungotevere dei Pierleoni or Piazza di Monte Savello.

The propylaeum of the Portico of Octavia contains the 8th-century church of *Sant'Angelo in Pescheria*, restored several times from the 16th century onwards. Unfortunately, the fine two-storey Romanesque bell tower, seen in early illustrations of the ghetto, collapsed around 1660. The present bell tower dates from the 19th century. It was in this church that the people's tribune Cola di Rienzo spent a night of prayer before launching his attack on the Capitol in 1347. During the last part of the ghetto's history, Jews attended the compulsory sermons in this church, when the community had obtained a reduction of such obligatory attendances to only two a year before the measure was abolished altogether by Pius IX in 1847. Intended to lead the Jews to 'see the light', these sermons had previously been held once a week, on Saturday, in the oratory of Trinità dei Pellegrini. The Jews present had initially numbered 100 men and 50

Via Rua with the Portico of
Ottavia in the background, 1886
(Archivio fotografico comunale)

Via delle Azzimelle, 1886
(Archivio fotografico comunale)

Lorenzo Manili's house (1468)
in Via del Portico d'Ottavia
with the words ad forum iudeorum

women, but as a result of a ruling by Clement VIII in 1592 these figures doubled. In the Jewish Museum there is a copy of a painting by Hieronimus Hess depicting the sermons: the bored, somnolent air of the congregation is hardly surprising, since before leaving the ghetto the Jews used to plug their ears with wax.

To the right of the Portico, in Via del Foro Piscario, is the stuccoed facade of the *Fishmongers' Oratory,* built in 1689 to house the Confraternity of Fishmongers; on the doorway is St Andrew, their patron saint.

At dawn on 16 October 1943, Nazi trucks arrived in the square in front of the Portico of Octavia and the SS began a series of raids on Jewish households. During that 'Black Saturday' over 1,000 men, women and children were seized. The event is recorded by a simple plaque on the facade of *Casa dei Vallati,* the 14th-century building at no. 29 now the City of Rome Ancient Monuments and Archaeology Department. Another inscription on the facade of Palazzo Salviati in Piazza della Rovere – now the Military College – recalls that the building was a prison for Jews before deportation to Auschwitz, a destination from which only 16 men and one woman returned.

With the Portico to your back, at the beginning of Via di Sant'Angelo in Pescheria you can get a fine view of what the ghetto must have been like – something akin to the image captured in those photographs just before the demolition work started, now in the City's Photography Archives (→ Itinerary VIII), or to the atmosphere in the watercolours by the Viennese artist Ettore Roesler Franz (1845-1907), who was fascinated by the ghetto and left an unrivalled pictorial account of its appearance (→ Itineraries III and VIII/*Museum of Rome* and *Museum of Roman Folklore*).

Pass down Via del Portico d'Ottavia, to the left of the Portico itself. The five, half-buried columns in the pavement indicate the width of the old Via di Pescaria, once lined on one side by the houses marking the limit of the 'Jew's Enclosure'. The 1555 enclosure was part blank wall, part inhabited buildings, and was put up in less than three months by 'His Holiness' architect' Salustio Peruzzi, son of the more famous Baldassare at a cost of 200 scudi and paid for by the Jews themselves.

The hasty implementation of the papal bull issued by Paul IV naturally caused a number of problems in the area: several churches had to be demolished or de-consecrated and various noble families – such as the Boccapaduli and the Baroncini – abandoned their palaces. The Branca, however, decided to stay in their palace in Piazza Giudea, adding the very significant suffix of 'de clausura' to their surname.

Initially there were two gateways to the ghetto – one giving onto the Portico of Octavia, the other onto Platea Judea. However, Du Pérac's 1577 map of the city shows a third gateway opposite the church of San Gregorio ai Quattro Capi, while a further two gateways were added in Via della Fiumara when Sextus V had the ghetto extended in 1589. This time the architect was Domenico Fontana, who had himself and his descendants appointed as permanent gatekeepers. The Jews of the ghetto had to pay an annual tribute of 2 gold ducats to Fontana and his descendants even after the gateway was demolished in 1848.

Moving beyond the 13th-century tower at no. 25 (the portal is framed with fragments of Roman architraves), you come to the 15th-16th-century *Casa dei Fabii* at no.13. The view of the porticoed courtyard and the first landing window gives you a good idea of what the multi-storey buildings of the demolished ghetto must have been like. Further down is the block between Via Sant'Ambrogio and Via della Reginella, included in the ghetto in 1823, when Leo XIII granted the Jews the right to live and open shops in the area.

At no. 5 Via della Reginella is an inscription on the facade indicating the *diretto dominio* – that is, the ownership – of the building belonging to the Confraternità del Santissimo Salvatore in Sancta Sanctorum (one of the oldest confraternities in Rome), but that the *utile dominio* – that is, occupation and use – of the buildings was granted to the Scola Nova, one of the five synagogues in the ghetto. Given that the Jews were forbidden to own property, the houses in the ghetto actually belonged to individual Christians or religious bodies. The right of tenancy was handed down from generation to generation thanks to the *jus gazagà*, a sort of perpetual tenancy, although at times individuals bequeathed the right to the synagogues.

The street culminates in Piazza Mattei with the *Turtle Fountain* (1581-84) made by Taddeo Landini to designs by Giacomo della Porta. This square was the site of one of three additional gateways to the ghetto opened in 1823 (the other two stood in Via di Pescaria).

At the end of Via del Portico d'Ottavia, on the left, stands the *Casa di Lorenzo Manili* (1468). Above the shops now occupying the ground floor you can still read the inscription – a dedication to himself and his descendants by a man imbued with humanism and Classical learning. The entire facade is covered with Greek and Roman archaeological remains: a stele decorated with four figures (from the Appian Way), an inscription from the shop of an *eborarius* (ivory-worker), a Greek stele decorated with a deer and fawn, and a fragment from a sarcophagus showing a lion gripping an antelope in its jaws. The inscription *Have Roma* placed above the windows giving onto Piazza Costaguti conveys Manili's love of ancient Rome. But even more interestingly, the inscription on the facade reveals the importance of the Jewish presence in this area at the height of the Renaissance, since it mentions that the building was constructed *ad*

G. Vasi, Piazza Giudia, 1747:
left, Lorenzo Manili's house;
right the ghetto entrance

forum judeorum, in the Jews' square. In fact, this is the site of the old Platea Judea, which was divided in two by one of the gateways to the ghetto and the junction of the two main roads through the ghetto – Via di Pescaria and Via Rua (the medieval Ruga Judeorum). Here, around the fountain designed by Giacomo della Porta in 1591 (moved to Piazza delle Cinque Scole in 1930), the little trade and business contacts allowed between Jew and Gentile took place. The general market included second-hand cloth stalls and craft shops; but come sunset (or an hour after sunset in summer), all contact between Jews and non-Jews had to cease. With a number of characteristic shops, today this piazza is the most Jewish of the Roman squares. One meeting place is the Boccione cakeshop (the name being one of those long-standing nicknames for individuals or entire families). Here you can try typical Jewish desserts and sweets, made from secret recipes handed down from generation to generation. Some of the original tastes and flavours of Ancient Rome survive in the use of spices, almond paste, and dried and candied fruit.

JEWISH CUISINE IN ROME

Like Roman cooking generally, traditional Jewish cuisine is basically humble fare with simple ingredients. Supplies in the ghetto were hard to come by and this was compensated by their imaginative use. Nowadays Jewish integration is so complete and cooking so much a part of Roman cuisine in general that it is difficult to pick out a 'typically Jewish' dish in Testaccio, Trastevere or in the Castelli area. The culinary tradition of the ghetto is still very much alive, and there are quite a few 'grandmother's recipes' now in Roman cuisine. As elsewhere, Jewish women showed great skill in adapting local traditions and ingredients to the culinary requirements of the *kasheruth* (i.e. avoiding the use of prohibited animals and the mixture of meat and milk products). Today, a number of the recipes they created

are associated with particular Jewish holidays and festivities.

Vegetables play an important part in Roman Jewish cooking. All parts of the greens are used in inventive recipes that often involve other vegetables or fish. Foremost amongst the fried vegetable dishes are: *carciofi alla giudia* – Roman artichokes deep-fried in oil after the outer leaves have been removed with a special knife; *pezzetti* – slices of various greens and root vegetables fried in batter; and *torzelli* – endive hearts, peppered and salted and deep-fried in oil. Other noteworthy recipes include lettuce served with beans and tomato sauce; *aliciotti con l'indivia* – anchovies baked with endives; *cicoria con la bottarga* – chicory with dried and pressed tuna or mullet spawn; and *concia* – fried courgettes marinated in oil, vinegar and basil, a speciality in all Roman Jewish households.

The inevitably frugal traditions of the ghetto are also reflected in the way meat is prepared and conserved, since even the fattiest part of the cut is used. Stews were prepared on the stove for hours and then left warm for the Sabbath meal. The windows around the Portico of Octavia were adorned with strips of cloth in the summer and strips of salted and peppered dried meat in the winter. This dried meat still features on the menu for Jewish feast days, along with tasty salami made with beef or goose meat. The nerves and odd cuts that could not be used in the preparation of these delicacies were used up in the preparation of a typical first course: *pasta e ceci e pennerelli* – pasta with a meat and chickpea sauce. Cold egg pasta is served with oil, peppers and herbs on the Sabbath, while one speciality for *Rosh Hashanah* (New Year) is *carcioncini* – beef or chicken ravioli served in broth. Fish occupies a special place in Roman Jewish cooking, perhaps due to the medieval fish market under the Portico of Octavia. A characteristic feast day dish is sweet and sour fish, probably a direct descendant from ancient Roman cuisine. *Confettini di*

Lenghi, Le Cinque Scole, *watercolour,*
1832 (Museo ebraico)

Piazza delle Cinque Scole, 1886,
(Archivio fotografico comunale)

ROME

mare are small red mullet marinated with pine nuts and raisins, while another celebrated dish is *baccalà in pastella* – stockfish fried in batter.

The influence of different countries, cultures and periods of history is most obvious in the dessert recipes, with their traces of Imperial Rome, Sephardic Spain and other Mediterranean areas. *Bollo* is a soft oval sponge (*pan di Spagna*) rich in raisins and candied fruit. A non-leavened version is eaten at Passover. The recipe is known to have been brought to Rome by the Jews expelled from Catalonia and Castille after 1492. Then there is a special sweet *pizza* of almonds, raisins, pine nuts and candied fruit, while *biscottini*, small biscuits, accompany the ancient ritual of *Mishmarah* (the vigil for circumcisions, barmitzvahs and weddings). A typical Passover dessert is *pizzarelle col miele* – mazzah doughnuts with raisins, pinenuts and cocoa. Mixed with sugar and eggs, the same dough is baked in the oven to form a traditional cake – the *pizza di mazzà*.

In 1989 the City Council initiated a conservation scheme for the ghetto following a feasibility study commissioned by the Lazio Regional Council. The aim was to consolidate and restore the buildings around the Portico of Octavia and in the area between Via Santa Maria del Pianto and Piazza delle Cinque Scole. Our itinerary now continues from this square named after the five historic synagogues. After the ghetto clearance in the early 20th century, the square was re-named Via del Progresso, but the original name was restored in the 1980s, at the prompting of the Jewish Cultural Centre. The fountain in the centre of the square once stood in Piazza Giudea. There is a fine view of the 16th-century *Palazzo Cenci-Bolgonetti* behind it, if you go some way up Monte Cenci. The story of the noble family that owned this palace is closely connected with the history of the Roman Jewish community. Alongside the *palazzo* is the church of *San*

Facade of the church of San Gregorio with the quote from Isaiah used against the Jews of the ghetto

Tommaso ai Cenci (begun in the 12th century). Cola di Rienzo was born near here in 1313, since his birthplace is described as being 'behind San Tommaso, near the Jews' Temple'. A plaque at the corner of Via San Bartolomeo dei Vaccinari commemorates his house, while 15th- and early 16th-century documents refer to the 'Jews' synagogue in Platea Mercatelli', built after the Trastevere temple had been destroyed by fire.

THE CINQUE SCOLE
The Scola Tempio in the Mercatello was the first place of Jewish worship in the city. Documents reveal that by 1518 it was already flanked by the Scola Nova. This also followed the Italian Rite (known as *Benè Roma*), adopted by various Italian Jewish communities and a direct descendant from the rite followed in Jerusalem. After the Spanish expulsions of 1492, this nucleus of *scole* was added to by synagogues for the Sephardim and Ashkenazim. Thus various *scole* came into being: Catalan, Aragonese, Castilian, Sicilian, French and German. In 1517, for example, the Catalan Jews acquired premises from the Cenci family for their synagogue and obtained official recognition for their temple from Leo X two years later. Various factors, however, ultimately led to the re-grouping of the synagogues: the decline in Rome's population after the sack of the city in 1527, the uneasy relations between the schools themselves and the increasingly rigid papal rulings concerning the community, such as Paul IV's bull forbidding the Jews to have more than one synagogue. By the end of the 16th century the five *scole* (the Catalana, Castigliana, Siciliana, Tempio and Nova) were all housed in one building, now no. 37, Piazza delle Cinque Scole. The right wing of the original structure, towards Via della Fiumara (the most unhealthy part of the ghetto, given its susceptibility to flooding), housed the Scola Castigliana and the Scola Tempio, while the left wing, with its distinctive clock tower, housed the

Scola Siciliana, the Scola Nova and the Scola Catalana. In the 17th and 18th centuries the building underwent various modifications, and in 1834-35 the facade was decorated with a Neoclassical aedicule attributed to Valadier. This was the last part of the ghetto to be demolished (1908-10), though a serious fire in 1893 had already destroyed the wooden interior of the Scola Tempio and had seriously damaged the Scola Castigliana.

Continuing down Lungotevere Cenci towards the present-day Temple, our tour of the ghetto comes to an end at the church of San *Gregorio alla Divina Pietà* (otherwise known as *San Gregorio ai Quattro Capi*). The 18th-century facade by Filippo Barigoni is decorated with a *Crucifixion* by the painter Etienne Parrocel. Below is an inscription in both Latin and Hebrew including a passage from Isaiah (65, 2-3): 'a rebellious people, which walketh in a way which was not good, after their own thoughts; a people that provoketh me to anger continually to my face'. This is a clear example of the use of biblical texts for anti-Jewish purposes in a church standing opposite two gateways into the ghetto.

Itinerary II: the Temple, the Spanish Temple and the Jewish Museum

THE TEMPLE
Designed by Vincenzo Costa and Osvaldo Armanni, the Temple was built between 1901 and 1904 on a site of 3,373 square metres – one of the four plots of land created by the ghetto clearance programme. The Jewish Community bought the plot from the City Council after thirteen years of tough negotiations, hampered by a crisis in both the economy in general and the property market in particular. The speech made at the inauguration of the Temple by the President of the Rome Community, Angelo Sereni, describes how thirty years after their emancipation, the Jews wanted a temple 'sited between

the Capitol and the Janiculum, between the monuments to Vittorio Emanuele II and Garibaldi, the two great architects of our united Italy; a majestically free Temple, surrounded by the pure and free light of the sun... the expression of liberty, equality and love.' Costa and Armanni did their best to translate this aspiration into an imposing landmark of 'severe and simple forms not without a certain moderate ornate richness, in perfect harmony with the forms of the other monuments in the city.'

Like the synagogues of Florence, Vercelli and Turin, the Rome Temple dates from the 'eclectic period', when architects had to invent their own style, as there were no ancient models for Jewish places of worship, earlier synagogues having been in houses in the ghetto. Thus the style chosen reflected contemporary taste, and the architects acknowledged that they had drawn their inspiration from 'the Greek style... directly influenced by Asian, and especially Assyrian motifs, subordinated to modern requirements'.

The building is formed of regular volumes surmounted by a pavilion cupola. The windows giving onto the women's galleries are in coloured glass and framed by two orders of half-columns. Although described as Doric and Ionic by the architects, these orders are actually very freely interpreted, with the addition of 'Assyrian' decorative elements. The facade giving onto Via del Tempio is divided by a crenellated frieze. In the lower part, four columns at the top of the entrance steps define the main doorway for one central and two side doors. The same layout is repeated above in the division of the large windows giving onto the women's galleries set between two bas-reliefs of palm branches, an element in the *lulav*. The facade culminates in a pediment decorated with the Tables of the Law, surmounted by a seven-branch candelabra.

The Temple is also a place of commemoration. The side of the building giving onto the Lungotevere bears four plaques: the first, unveiled in the

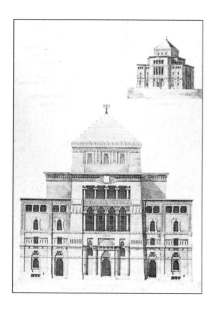

Design of the Temple
by V. Costa and O. Armanni, 1899
(Archivio Comunità ebraica di Roma)

The Temple

ROME

*The Temple interior in the design
by V. Costa and O. Armanni, 1900*

The Temple interior seen
from the women's gallery

ROME

The bimah *and* aron *in the Temple*

presence of King Vittorio Emanuele III and Marshall Diaz in 1921, is dedicated to the Roman Jewish soldiers who died in the First World War; the other three are placed alongside the doorway and commemorate the victims of 16 October 1943, of the Fosse Ardeatine, and fifteen partisans and anti-fascists who died in Rome (including Leone Ginzburg and Eugenio Colorni). The most recent inscription, on the gatepost of the Via Catalana entrance, commemorates the young Stefano Gaj Taché, killed during the terrorist attack which wounded a further forty worshippers as they left the Temple after the *Shemini Azeret* service on 9 October 1982, all struck down by 'the hands of killers driven by anti-semitic hatred'.

The visitors' entrance for the Temple, the Museum and the Community offices (in the apse of the building) is in Lungotevere Cenci. Guided visits to the Temple and Museum start every half-hour from 9 am to 5 pm (Monday to Thursday) and 9 am to 12.30 pm (Friday and Sunday). Booking is advised for group visits (tel. 02/6840061). On request, the Museum also organises visits to the ghetto.

A first glimpse on entering the Temple immediately conveys the effect of the sumptuous decoration, the massive columns and the lofty cupola. The internal layout is a slightly elongated Greek cross, reflecting the external ground-plan of the building. On three sides a colonnade supports the women's galleries while separating the main part of the hall from the two side aisles and the main entrance behind the external portico. Against the wall facing you on entering is the *aron* (ark), This is a very ornate aedicule with six Assyrian-style columns with gilded volutes and friezes, surmounted by an architrave and a pediment. The Tables of the Law above bear the inscription 'Holy for the Lord. Know before Whom you stand'. The *aron* rests on the *bimah* (podium); this is approached by two side flights of eight steps surrounded by an iron

Detail of the Temple interior

balustrade with marble panels. The design of *aron* and *bimah* is typical of the synagogues of the period just after emancipation, and was clearly inspired by the layout of catholic churches, with the altar marking a clear separation between celebrant and congregation. In the original Cinque Scole, as in the Venetian synagogues (→ *Venice and surroundings Jewish Itineraries*), the *aron* and *bimah* were placed opposite each other and the benches for the congregation set on the axis between them. This more satisfactorily reflected the Jewish tradition whereby all participants in *tefillah* (collective prayer) are equal and directly involved.

The *aron* and *bimah* stand in a semi-hexagonal apse: the walls at the level of the women's gallery are decorated with ornate panels bearing large gilded seven-branch candelabra and medallions. The numerous biblical quotations adorning the walls, pilasters and outer doorways were chosen by Rabbi Vittore Castiglioni, the author of an elegy in Hebrew and Italian written for the inauguration of the Temple. Castiglioni's elegy is in the tradition of Hebrew liturgical poetry in Rome going back to the Middle Ages. A plaque to the right of the entrance commemorates the visit made by Emanuele III on 2 July 1904, just a few weeks before the Temple was inaugurated.

The four corners of the cupola drum rest on brackets and full-voluted capitals surmounting columns in turn resting on large fluted pilasters. The women's galleries are enclosed by iron balustrades decorated with small lamps and lit by large windows of multi-coloured Art-Nouveau-style glass. The work of Annibale Brugnoli and Domenico Bruschi, the interior decoration consists of rich stucco-work and Oriental-style paintings of tapestries on walls and ceilings with starry skies. The inner surface of the cupola is aluminium, thus enhancing the luminescence of the painted rainbow-coloured scales rising above the square-shaped lantern. The base of each quarter segment of the cupola, however, is decorated with palm trees and Lebanese cedars, reflecting Jewish symbolism and the Oriental influence in the decoration.

The Temple houses many of the artistic treasures of the original Cinque Scole and thus marks the continuity between past and present. The Jews of Rome are specially fond of these precious furnishings, fabrics and artefacts. The marble furnishings from the old *scole* (seats, arks, pulpits, columns and basins) were, in many cases, re-positioned according to strictly functional or decorative criteria rather than in their original arrangements. Most of the furnishings date from the 16th and 17th century and were made in various polychrome marbles according to the taste of the period.

In 1937 two arks from the historic *scole* were installed at the head of the two side aisles of the Temple; the *aron* in the right aisle came from the Scola Siciliana, that in the left from the Scola Castigliana. The 'Sicilian' *aron* columns, made of Sciro breccia, support the architrave with the Tables of the Law and the pediment bearing the *menorah*. This *aron* can be dated thanks to the Hebrew inscription which reads: 'Holy for the Lord. Scola Siciliana, Year 5346' (1586). The gilded wooden doors are 19th-century, and the interior panels depict the Tabernacle and ritual articles as described in the Torah.

The 'Castilian' *aron* has similarities with the tabernacles produced for the churches of the time (see, for example, that in Sant'Agostino): the broken pediment resting on columns, along with the use of different marbles and geometric inlays. The Hebrew inscriptions commemorate the offerings made by the Corcos and Coen families for various parts of the furnishings of the Scola Castigliana (the first offering dates from 1642). The last such inscription dates from 1937, when Enrico Coen paid for the relocation of these two *aronoth* and their chairs to the modern Temple.

The dome interior

Detail of the windows

Temple interior, the aron
from the Scola Castigliana, 1642-1660

Temple interior, the aron
from the Scola Castigliana, 1586

Made between 1642 and 1660 thanks to an offering by David Viterbo, the chair that originally stood alongside the Castilian *aron* was ultimately set at the right-hand side of the *bimah* in the Temple, while on the left is the 1586 chair from the Sicilian *aron* – an inscription under the crest records the offering made by the Di Tivoli family. At the same time the *bimah* was also adorned with five double brass candelabra from the Catalan and Castilian *scole*.

In 1938 an antique basin was relocated alongside one of the entrances giving onto the Lungotevere. The use of polychrome marble and inlays in the basin decoration once echoed that in the Castilian *aron*. But the present basin seems to be a combination of parts from different sources. The wall behind it is decorated with a large engraved shell above lines from Isaiah (12,3): 'with joy draw waters out of the wells of salvation'. The inscription above these lines records an offering made by Yehuda Bises in 1642.

Other furnishings from the Cinque Scole have been re-assembled in the lower rooms of the Temple, which were refurbished in 1955 by the architect Angelo Di Castro for recreational, social and cultural uses. Opposite the staircase to the lower rooms is the imposing chair made in 1623 for the *aron* in the Scola Nova. Again the use of different kinds of marble is a key decorative feature. The inscription on the pediment recalls those who made the offering for the chair: Shabbetai, son of Ghershom Di Segni and Mordekhai, son of Yosef Toscano. Moving down the corridor, on the left you pass the four imposing marble Corinthian columns from the Scola Castigliana, while on the right are three large plaques with the details of bequests. This was quite common practice among the Jews of the ghetto, given that the religious, educational and social services offered by the *scole* and confraternities could only be funded by individual offerings. The first two inscriptions are in Hebrew

Temple basement, the chair from the Scola Nova, 1623

with a summary in Italian. They record an 1857 bequest in favour of the *Ozer Dallim* Confraternity ('Help the Needy') from the Modigliani, complete with the official registration by the notary Vitti, and an 1855 bequest in favour of the Scola Siciliana from the Genazzano, registered by the same notary. The third inscription, only in Hebrew, records the 1854 bequest of 1,000 scudi for the poor of the Scola Siciliana made by Shelomo Yehuda Bonaventura and registered by the notary Blasi. A condition for the bequest was that the poor commemorate their benefactor and his wife Hanna with prayers and candles. The far wall is decorated with other furnishings from the historic *scole*. These include a marble plaque, at the top left of the wall, with the inscription 'Holy for the Lord by the congregation of the Scola Tempio' – one of the few items to have survived the fire that destroyed that synagogue. The circular plaque to the right bears a similar inscription and comes from the Scola Catalana, while the large plaque at the centre of the wall bears a quote from Psalms (5,8) and probably came from the entrance to one of the *scole*.

In 1995, the Superintendence for Architectural Heritage started work on re-assembling the surviving fragments of the *Aron from the Scola Catalana* in the entrance to the lower rooms. Attempts to make the *aron* functional again have run into difficulties due to its height. It is, however, the oldest extant ark in Italy, and certainly the most valuable remnant from the Cinque Scole. Made in white and purple Carrara marble, the *aron* suggests that when the Catalan Jews arrived in Rome after the 1492 expulsions they had the economic means to settle in the city and almost immediately – that is, in 1519 – found a *scola* of their own (the Mercatello synagogue), which they furnished with a costly *aron*, whose Mannerist style reflects Roman taste at the time. The surviving fragments reveal that the architrave, frieze, pediment and door-

Temple basement, the aron *from the Scola Catalana, 1523*

frame all had gilding, while the door was surmounted by an inscription taken from the Book of Numbers (31,54), and containing the date in the word *zikkaron*, marked by apostrophes. The Tables of the Law in the pediment are flanked by two trumpets and stand out against a sea-blue background. The Neoclassical-style doors are gilded and their inner panels depict the ritual articles as described in the Pentateuch. The central part of the base with wooden doors has been lost – as has one of the two lion-head pilasters supporting the columns. The *aron* stood at the top of three semi-circular white Carrara marble steps whose remains are now in the Temple garden.

THE SPANISH TEMPLE

At the end of the corridor, the door on the right leads to the Spanish Temple. The doorway itself is decorated with three of the marble inlays which used to adorn the floors of the Cinque Scole. The Spanish Temple originally occupied a building on the Lungotevere Sanzio constructed between 1908 and 1910. Also designed by Costa and Armanni, this building stood on a lot obtained by the Community in exchange for the demolition of the building with the Cinque Scole and the ceding of that site to Rome City Council. Thus, the Sephardim, who had for centuries worshipped according to their own rite in their own synagogue, could keep their traditions alive, alongside the Italian rite celebrated in the new 1904 Temple and now followed by most of the Jewish community. The Spanish Temple building also contained an elementary school, and due to growing scholastic needs, the temple was transferred to its present location in 1932. In 1948 the temple was refurbished and adorned with furnishings taken from the Cinque Scole.

The Spanish Temple best evokes the atmosphere of the historic *scole*, both because of the design of the space and the layout of the furnishings. The synagogue has two 'focal

The aron *and chairs from the Scola Catalana, 1886 (Archivio fotografico comunale)*

*The Spanish Temple, crest
of Jeuda Iair, 1646*

The Spanish Temple, the aron
*from the Scola Nova and
the chairs from the Scola Catalana*

points': the *aron* and *tevah* facing each other in the middle of the side walls. A similar layout can be seen in the Mantua synagogue, for example (→ *Lombardy Jewish Itineraries*). The *aron* came from the Scola Nova and, for reasons of space, was reassembled without the upper part of the pediment, which was placed above the first stone testamentary plaque in the corridor. The style and variegated marble of the *aron* are similar to those in the Castilian *aron*, dating from the same period and now located in the Temple. One variant in the Spanish *aron* are the fluted and inlaid side columns. The square-panelled doors are in gilded wood. The chair previously beside the Scola Nova *aron* has already been described and can be seen in the entrance hall; the two very fine purple marble chairs now flanking the ark came from the *aron* in the Scola Catalana. This arrangement of two chairs and ark is similar to that in the 1543 Mantua-Sermide *aron* and chairs (now in Jerusalem) and that in the Scuola Canton and Scuola Tedesca in Venice (→ *Venice and surroundings Jewish Itineraries*). The seats date from when the Scola Catalan was enlarged (1622-28) by Girolamo Rainaldi with the aid of Francesco Peparelli. The inscription on the left-hand chair commemorates the donor, David, son of Shemuel Gattegna, and is dated 1623. The traditional inscription in the pediment reads: 'Crown of the Torah'. The non-original panel in the right-hand chair records that the restoration of these furnishings in 1948 was made possible by the Limentani family. Not on the original chair, the crest on the pediment (1646) is an open-tailed peacock and bears an inscription to Jehuda Iair. On the sides of the ark are two other testamentary plaques both recording bequests to the Scola Castigliana: the one on the right is dated 1836 and records the legacy from the Sonnino family, that on the left the legacies in the period 1796-1852 from the Modigliani, Corcos, Spizzichino and Esdra families.

The Spanish Temple: fountain with an inscription of 1624 concerning the Scola Catalana

The white marble *tevah* (1851) comes from the Scola Castigliana. The inscription commemorates the donors, the Modigliani family. The backs of the wooden pews bear the names of those who donated these furnishings to commemorate the victims of Nazi deportation and of the Fosse Ardeatine massacre. The vestibule of the Spanish Temple gives directly onto the garden; the fountain and water basin is a collage of pieces from different historical periods: the inscription plaque (with the date 1624 and the name of the Scola Catalana-Aragonese) is from the same period as the basin, while the columned section and the frame are in Cosmati work (the two trapezophora in the form of lion's claws are difficult to date, one has clearly been re-worked). Opposite the Spanish Temple, the outer walls of the garden are decorated with plaques and marble fragments with furnishings that once adorned the Cinque Scole and the Confraternities. There are testamentary plaques, commemorative inscriptions, fountains and collection boxes from various periods. Interestingly some of the inscriptions are in 'squared Hebrew', the script used by the Sephardic community, although here it is often embellished to form the so-called 'floriated Hebrew'. Returning to the underground rooms, note to the left the door leading to the small women's gallery: there are still traces of the seals placed by the Nazis in 1943.

The marble plaque (1725) was originally above an *aron* chair in the Scola Castigliana; the Hebrew verses commemorate the restoration of the chair at the behest of Shemual Corcos (son of the famous rabbi, Manoach Hizkiya – Tranquillo Vita Corcos, 1659-1730) and Yosef Chayat. On the side is an 1865 plaque of the Talmud Torah.

THE JEWISH MUSEUM

It takes at least three quarters of an hour to visit this major museum documenting the historical, cultural and artistic heritage of the ghetto. The large collections include ritual objects, precious fabrics, various documents, manuscripts and incunabula as well as the archives and surviving furnishings from the Cinque Scole. Created in 1960 through the efforts of Fausto Pitigliani and designed by Roberto Pontecorvo, the museum originally occupied a single room. Then a new ground floor room was opened in 1995 (the restoration and conversion being paid for by the Sonnino family, in memory of Samuele and Bianca Sonnino). In keeping with the wishes of the Rome community, the museum maintains its character as the 'wardrobe of the Temple': the objects and fabrics on display are in regular use in the various synagogues (their state of preservation permitting), so there is a regular turn-over in the objects on display in the showcases. This is the Italian Jewish museum which receives the largest number of school visits, playing host to an average of four classes a day of all ages.

UPPER ROOM

On the right wall of the stairs leading up to the room there are some plaster casts of inscriptions to be found in the Jewish catacombs (→ Itinerary IX). The glass in the five windows is the work of Eva Fischer (1981) and depicts Rome, Jerusalem, Hebron, Tiberias and Safed; the sixth window, at the end of the room, depicts the *berachah*, the traditional paternal blessing bestowed upon children. Made in 1760 by Gaspare Vannechi and donated to the Scola Tempio by Giuseppe Vivanti, the large silver candelabra has three orders of lights. The walls of the upper room contain a display of documents: decrees, announcements and edicts, complete with reproductions of prints and engravings, concerning life in the ghetto. The showcase in front of the window contains some parchment manuscripts from the Community library, including a Pentateuch from the early 15th century (once in the Scola Nova), and a codex containing the

Jewish Museum, upper room

ROME

Pentateuch, the Books of the Prophets and the Hagiographa, acquired by the Scola Tempio in 1569 from Elishah, son of Shabbetai of Terracina. The central showcase has records of the more recent past. They include the report by the Community President Ugo Foà on Nazi plundering in 1943, the receipts issued for the gold collected, the prison records of Jews interned in the prisons of Via Tasso (→ Itinerary VI) and a prayer book pierced by the shrapnel of a bomb thrown into the crowd of worshippers leaving the synagogue on 9 October 1982. On the end wall is a marble inlay from the floor in front of the *aron* of the Scola Siciliana. It is, in fact, a 17th-century Florentine tabletop in mosaic and soft stones. Here and in the room below, the heritage of the Cinque Scole is organised in the showcases according to themes. This is the major attraction at the museum and makes it one of the most important of its kind in Europe. The fabrics and silverware almost all date from the 17th to 19th century. They reveal that the Jewish patrons were very knowledgeable about silver-smithing and fabric weaving – all the more remarkable, given the difficult economic conditions in the ghetto. The donations of this material to the *scole* – often also a way of avoiding extra papal taxes – is symptomatic of a social climate in which even the less wealthy families considered it an honour to employ their limited means in the decoration of their synagogue.

Trade and moneylending – as well as the issue of 'travel licences' for other cities in the Papal States – meant that the community was not restricted to local manufacturers when it came to acquiring material for their synagogues. But, as in Tuscany and the Veneto, the Jews had to resort to Christian silversmiths for their commissions, and they used some of the most noted craftsmen of their day. The fabrics, on the other hand, demonstrate the skilled needlework by the ghetto women in the various precious damasks, velvets and lampasses.

Manuscript containing the Pentateuch, *the* Prophets *and the* Hagiographa *acquired by the Scola Tempio in 1569 from Elisha, son of Shabbatai da Terracina*

Receipt for 9 grams of gold, part of the 50 kilos demanded from the Rome Community by the German High Command in 1943

Detail of the embroidery on a mappah
with the crest of the Ascarelli family,
Scola Catalana, 1770

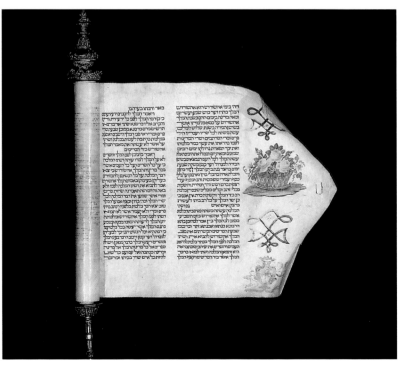

Rimmonim *and crown, Scola Catalana,*
Venice 1730 - Rome 1767

Scroll containing the Book of Esther
(Megillath Esther) *written and*
illuminated by Yacov Zoref da
Castelnuovo, 1633

Marriage contract (ketubah) *of*
Biniamin Amati and Simha Sestieri,
Rome, 1795

Among the most striking exhibits in the upper room are the large ornamental curtains (*parocheth*) and pulpit covers (*tikkunei ha-tevah*) used to decorate the furnishings of the *scole*. The *parocheth* in the middle of the left wall is well worthy of note: made of 15th-century Florentine material, it was donated to the *Scola Catalana* in 1703 by Yehuda Malakh. Dating from the end of the 16th century, the striking pulpit cover above the entrance is decorated with flowers and birds set in a silver background. On the left hand wall there is also a red satin *mappah*, the ceremonial cover for the Torah. Decorated at the centre with a large crest and dedication embroidered in gold (16th-century Florentine work), it was donated to Scola Tempio by the Zaddik family. In the third case on the right there are two complete sets of adornments for the Torah: cloak (*meil*), sash, crown (*keter* or *atarah*), half-crown (*tass*) and ferrules (*rimmonim*). Some of these pieces were donated to the Scola Tempio at the turn of the 19th century by the Mieli – note the family emblem of bees on a barrel of honey (*miele* in Italian) – others were donated to the Scola Nuova in the first half of the 18th century by the Alatri family. Alongside, you cannot help but notice the silver *rimmonim* begun in Venice around 1730 and completed in Rome in 1767 by Giuseppe Bartolotti. Their Baroque form of niches and barley-sugar columns bring to mind Bernini's baldacchino in St Peter's. Downstairs is a similar work from 1777-79 by Bartolotti's son, Carlo.

The last case in the upper room contains some parchment scrolls of the Book of Esther (*Megillath Esther*) – including a manuscript written and illuminated in 1633 by Yacov Zoref from Castelnuovo – and the lamps (*ner tamid*) which always hung alight before the *aron* (of various dates and styles). The first two cases on the right contain bowls and jugs used for the ceremonial washing of hands by the members of the rabbinical family

Hanukkiah, *Scola Nova, by silversmith Pietro Zappati, Rome, 1761-63*

Basins, Scola Catalana, by goldsmith Corinzio Colleoni, Rome, 1612-18

Jewish Museum: lower room

Ornamental cape for the Torah (meil)
with decoration depicting the Temple
of Jerusalem, Scola Siciliana Venice,
18th century

(*kohanim*) before the solemn communal benediction, and various *hannukioth*. Amongst the bowls, note the one with the ewer in the form of a lion bearing a shield with the crest of the donor family, the Tedeschi. This rare piece of 17th-century Flemish-German embossed silverwork was once in the *Scola Catalana*. Note also the complete set of gilded silver vessels made by the Roman goldsmith Corinzio Colleoni in the early 17th century. The three large wall *hannukioth* in embossed silver are particularly striking: one is the work of Francesco Teoli (1710-19) and comes from the Scola Catalana, the other two were made in the mid 18th century by Pietro Zappati and come from the Scola Castigliana and the Scola Nova. Above the showcases are some 18th- and 19th-century parchment marriage contracts (*ketubboth*) written and decorated in Rome. Note the typical triangular form of the lower side, required for tying up the scroll with a ribbon before presenting it to the bride's mother.

THE LOWER ROOM

Two sides of the lower room have hanging display cases containing a hundred or so of the *meilim* used to cover the scrolls of the Torah. Many are in vividly-coloured precious fabrics – such as the early to mid 17th-century cape in blue silk embroidered with coloured silk and gold thread from the Scola Siciliana and probably cut from a bridal gown, or the red silk velvet cape decorated with embroidery work in green and blue silk and thread-of-gold depicting ritual furnishings described in the Pentateuch. Underneath, the five showcases contain silver ferrules (*rimmonim*) for the scrolls of the Torah, often exhibited together with crowns. The former are mainly in the traditional 'tower' and 'pomegranate' design of Sephardic origin very widespread in Italy. However, there are examples of other designs, such as the so-called 'thimble' and 'vase' designs. Each is richly decorated, to meet the Roman taste of the

day, and adorned with pomegranates, bells and pendants that tinkle with each movement of the *sefer*. Amongst the oldest are the gilded silver 'thimble' ferrules donated to the Scola Tempio in 1638 by Raffaele De' Rossi (the lower rim is set with turquoises), and the pair of globular ferrules surmounted by lions, donated to the Scola Catalana in 1651 by Ora Natronai.

The showcases on the end wall contain some complete sets of Torah adornments, including that donated to the Scola Tempio by the Sereni family in 1723-24: the imposing *rimmonim* are surmounted by a cockerel, the symbol of the donor family, also found in the fringe of the cape. In the showcase alongside note the *meil* in blue silk almost entirely covered with gold embroidery depicting the Temple in Jerusalem. This 18th-century Venetian work was donated to the Scola Siciliana by Isacco Corcos. The corner showcase contains the silver Tables of the Law once on the pediments of the arks in the Scola Nova and Scola Tempio (19th century), along with two large covered chalices in embossed silver dating from the end of the 18th century, used for the *qiddush* in the synagogues. The centre of the room contains a chronologically-arranged display of the hands (*yad*) used in the readings from the Torah. The oldest dates from 1612 and was given to the Scola Nova by Fiore Di Segni; but the collection also includes the *yad* made from a coral branch (the silver handle is by Bernardino Birelli) donated to the Scola Nova by Giuseppe Baraffael in 1765, and a *yad* in the form of a palm branch borne aloft by two lions, the work of Gaspare Vanneschi (1770-72).

In the showcases alongside you can see some 18th- and 19th-century prayer books (*machzorim*) bound in silver, or velvet and silver, often with family crests on both covers. These books were usually wedding gifts. Opposite is a display of ancient books, prints and incunabula, including three rare Soncino editions: *Sefer*

Complete set gifted by the Sereni family to the Scola Tempio, 1723-24

Three pointers for reading the Torah (yad)*, Rome, 18th century*

Curtain for the ark (parocheth),
Scola Nova, Venice, 18th century

Elijah's chair used for circumcision

Ha 'Iqqarim ('The Book of the Fundamentals') by Yosef Albo (1485), the *Machzor Ke-Minhag Benè Roma*, a collection of prayers for the Roman or Italian rite (c. 1500), the 1517 *Sefer 'Arukh* ('Ordered Book') by Rabbi Nathan ben Yechiel (c. 1035-1106) and a book probably published in Rome around 1469-72 – the *Sefer Ha-Shorashim* ('The Book of Roots') by Rabbi David Qimchi (1160-1235).

The case beneath the windows contains various objects traditionally associated with ritual celebrations: the hammer for pounding kosher meat, the silver instruments for circumcision (*milah*), the coins used to ransom the first-born (*pidyion haben*), the silver and filigree medallions (*shaddai*) hung on cots to protect babies – all dating from the 18th and 19th century. One curious item is the unusually large glass beaker for the *panata* – a pap given to women after childbirth to improve the quality of their milk. Between the windows are two large 19th-century chairs of the prophet Elijah, which were carried to individual houses for circumcisions. In the two showcases alongside the door are a collection of chalices used for the *qiddush*, plus spice pots (*besamim*) and cups for citron (*etrog*). Dating from various periods and in different styles, these objects complete the collection of silverware used in domestic rituals.

In the entrance vestibule of the Museum and Temple there is a lift up to the upper floors. On the third floor are the Community offices, on the second a conference room and the Rabbi's offices. The study of the chief rabbi contains an old walnut cabinet from the confraternities in the ghetto (the name or symbol is carved in Hebrew characters on the panels), a collection of 18th-and 19th-century Roman parchment *ketubboth* decorated with geometric and floral motifs, and a silver Tables of the Law made by the goldsmith Angelo Giannotti in the first half of the 19th century and donated by the Citone family to the Scola

Siciliana, where it adorned the *aron*. The Temple building also contains a library of manuscripts, incunabula, and rare editions of Bible texts, ritual texts and prayer books (some on display in the museum) and a historic archive recognised in 1981 as being 'of noteworthy interest' by the Superintendent of State Archives. The Archives themselves contain documentation concerning the life of the Jews in the ghetto, including the records of the *Vaad* (Council) and of the *scole* and confraternities. For further information, contact the Jewish Community of Rome (tel. 06/6840061).

THE JEWISH-ROMAN DIALECT

Visitors to the old ghetto area may still hear among the stalls around the Temple or near the Portico of Ottavia an accent or expressions that vary from the usual Roman dialect. This Jewish-Roman accent has been kept alive by its household use and various cultural activities (theatre and courses). Up to the second half of the 16th century, the Roman Jews spoke the common language of the city – perhaps adding a few Hebrew terms here and there, most referring to their religious or professional life. We get a vivid idea of how they spoke from written records of 16th-century trials with Jews as either defendants or witnesses. After the ghetto was enclosed in 1555, the two vernaculars developed in different directions. The advent of Florentine popes meant that Tuscan began to have a great effect on the dialect of Rome itself, which thus gradually lost its southern roots. At the same time the enclosure in the ghetto meant that the Jewish-Roman dialect developed undisturbed. Indeed, its southern connotations were reinforced with the arrival of refugees from southern Italy. The use of Hebrew words in common parlance increased as language became a means of 'self-defence', preventing papal 'spies' from eavesdropping on conversations.

There are numerous southern features in Jewish-Roman dialect: for example, the sounding of the dental 't' in the feminine plural (*berakhot*, 'blessings' becomes *berachodde*, with a double, Italian and Hebrew, plural); 'io ho' [I have] becomes '*aio*', 'Mondo' *munno*, and 'secondo' *secunno*, and so on. There is also a typical form of the possessive: *madrema*, *patreto* and *figlievi* for 'mia madre', 'tuo padre' and 'i vostri figli' respectively. Moreover, in Jewish Roman the plural of female nouns often takes the masculine (e.g. *i busti* for 'le buste'). The Jewish dialect also has two sounds not found in Italian: the Hebrew vowel *ain* (*ngkain* in the typical Roman Jewish pronunciation) and the *chedd* sound. The first sound is a kind of strongly nasal *ng* used in Hebrew words (*ngkavon* - 'sin') and in the pronunciation of certain Italian words (*snagkue* - 'sangue'). The latter is a heavily aspirated *h*-sound, as in *chatan* [bridegroom] and *Pesach* [Passover].

In 1868, just two years before the total emancipation of the ghetto, the most celebrated Jewish-Roman poet was born – Crescenzo Del Monte. A passionate scholar of both Roman and Jewish-Roman traditions, an admirer of Belli and a student of Jewish-Roman dialects, Del Monte published two collections of sonnets: *Sonetti giudaico-romaneschi* (1927) and *Nuovi sonetti giudaico-romaneschi* (1935). In 1955, almost twenty years after his death (1936) his *Sonetti postumi* were published. An anthology of these three collections was published in 1977 by Beniamino Carucci, but is now very difficult to obtain.

Itinerary III: Ponte Quattro Capi, the Isola Tiberina and Trastevere

PONTE QUATTRO CAPI

Linking the Lungotevere Cenci and the Isola Tiberina opposite the Temple, the Ponte Fabricio (62 BCE) is also known as 'Four Heads Bridge' because of the four marble herms incorporated into its parapets. In the Middle Ages it was known as the *Pons Judeorum*, a name which first appeared in the 11th century, and in various

ous documents is explained with the comment *quia ibi Judaei habitant*, 'because the Jews live there'. The bridge gave its name to a medieval synagogue nearby, the Scola dei Quattro Capi. But in 1558 the *scola* in what was known as the 'ghettarello' – the area towards Monte Savello on the boundary of the ghetto proper, previously not affected by the segregation rules – had to move. Following its merger with the Scola Porta or Portaleone, located in the same area, the Scola dei Quattro Capi continued to function first as an oratory and then as a confraternity associated with the Cinque Scole. The empty premises of this synagogue are mentioned by the Jewish traveller Abramo Levi in 1724. A silver crown, dated 1626 and donated by the Del Monte family, together with part of a 1670 ark curtain (*parocheth*) are now in the Jewish Museum.

THE ISOLA TIBERINA

This island marks the meeting point between the Jewish settlements on either side of the Tiber – that is, between the Trastevere community (sizeable in Roman and medieval times, and still active in the first decades of the 16th century) and the Sant'Angelo community in the area between the Portico of Octavia and the Platea Judea, in continual expansion since the institution of the ghetto.

Shaped like a stone ship, the island was once clad and decorated with marble, of which some traces survive. In ancient times it was the site of an important temple dedicated to Aesculapius, and today it still houses medical facilities: the Fatebenefratelli Hospital and the offices and clinics of the Jewish Hospital. It is also the site of the *Panzieri-Fatucci Oratory*, or Temple of the Young (entrance at no. 21, Piazza San Bartolomeo).

The Jewish Hospital was created when, after the 1870 liberation, two confraternities previously active in the ghetto – the *Bikkur Cholim* and *Moshav Zeqenim* – decided to join forces and set up the first social services for the emancipated Jewish community:

*The Ponte Quattro Capi
and the Isola Tiberina*

ROME

The Panzieri-Fatucci Oratory
or Temple of the Young

the Ospedale Israelitico and the Rico-
vero Israeliti Poveri Invalidi. In 1937,
a year before the approval of the Fascist Race laws, an oratory for the Old
People's Home was opened. Little did
the two-thousand-year-old community know that during the dark days
to come this small room would guar-
antee the continuance of their religious life during the nine months of
Nazi occupation. As a plaque inside
commemorates, this was the only synagogue which continued functioning
clandestinely after the seals had been
set on all the other places of worship –
largely due to the courage of Rabbi
David Panzieri. And it was here that
the Jews of the Roman Community
and those serving with the American
Fifth Army prayed together on the
morning of 5 June 1944. After the war
the oratory was renamed in honour of
David Panzieri and Amadio Fatucci
(the latter a victim at the Fosse
Ardeatine) and continued to function
until the new Hospital and Old People's Home were opened in the Maglia-
na district (no. 14 Via Fulda) in 1970.
Completely renovated in 1987, on the
Sabbath and feast days it is a Temple of
the Young, who have thus been entrusted with continuing this part of the
community's traditions.

The small room on the top floor
contains a wooden *aron* dating from
1897. Once in the Cinque Scole building, it was probably used after the fire
in the Scola Tempio. The pulpit (*tevah*)
dates from 1937. The brightly-col-
oured stained-glass windows (1988),
depicting the tribes of Israel and the
various Jewish feasts, and the grate enclosing the women's gallery (1995) are
all the work of Aldo Di Castro.

TRASTEVERE
The Ponte Cestio leads from the island
over to Trastevere. Moving beyond Piazza in Piscinula (note the 14th-15th-
century *Palazzo dei Mattei*) down to
the end of Via in Piscinulam, you come
to Via dei Salumi. Crossing the road,
you reach Vicolo dell'Atleta. Here the
building at no. 14 is commonly held to
have housed the old synagogue of

*The medieval synagogue
in Vicolo dell'Atleta*

ROME

Trastevere – written accounts by 19th-century travellers and historians all locate the synagogue somewhere amongst these buildings. The identification is possibly borne out by the Hebrew inscription (*Nathan Chai*) on the column supporting the two arches of the loggia, and by the presence of a well in the building itself. We do not know which Nathan the inscription refers to, but at the turn of the 12th century the rabbi and lexicologist Nathan ben Yechiel (c. 1035-1106) founded a synagogue and ritual baths in Trastevere. He also wrote the *Sefer 'Arukh* ('Ordered Book'), a Talmudic dictionary listing all the terms in post-biblical literature in alphabetical order, an important work of reference for ritual worship in the temple.

Among the eminent community figures Benjamin of Tudela met during his 1159-67 visit to Rome were the grandson of Rabbi Nathan, Rabbi Yechiel, administrator of Pope Alexander III's estates and expressly referred to as 'living in Trastevere'. Both were members of the Anaw family. One of the most ancient and famous Jewish families in Rome, the Anaw contributed some of the community's illustrious doctors, writers, translators and copyists in the 13th and 14th centuries. Another member of the family, Rabbi Yechiel, son of Yechutiel, was a writer and religious poet. He wrote an elegy commemorating a fire in a synagogue (probably in Trastevere) on 7 Elul 5028 (28 August 1268). Many sacred furnishings and 21 scrolls of the Law were lost in the fire, which was commemorated in the community by a day of fasting and penance for many years to come.

A year earlier another catastrophe had hit the Jewish community: the ancient cemetery, located in the Porta Portese area between the church of San Francesco a Ripa and the present-day Piazza Bernardino da Feltre, had been vandalised and profaned. This event is recorded in a penitential poem (*selichah*) written by Rabbi Binyamin ben Avraham Anaw.

Funerary inscription of Domnus Arconte, Catacomba di Monteverde, Ospizio di San Cosimato

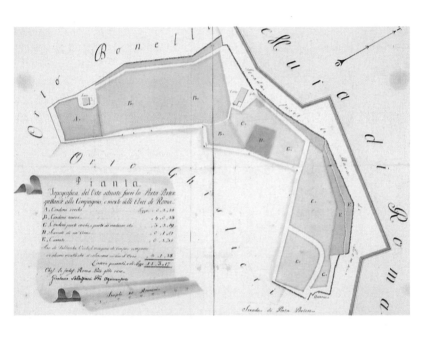

Map of the Porta Portese Jewish Cemetery (Archivio della Comunità ebraica di Roma)

B. Pinelli, The tournament of hunchback Jews, *1828 (Museo del folklore e dei poeti romaneschi)*

The *campus judeorum* or 'Jews' Yard' mentioned in the 1363 Rome Statutes was used as a place of burial up to 1645, when the Confraternity *Ghemilut Chasadim* ('Charity and Death'), which had the papal licence to run the burial-ground, procured a new cemetery site on the Aventine (→ Itinerary IV). Various 16th-century Hebrew inscriptions from the tombs (mostly on the top of Roman capitals or recycled marble cippi) can now be seen in various locations: some – such as those in the cloister of San Giovanni in Laterano (→ Itinerary VI) and the Capitoline Museum (→ Itinerary V) – can be seen during the course of an ordinary visit, others – such as those in the courtyard of the Banca d'Italia (no. 91 Via Nazionale), in the Celio Antiquarium (Villa Celimontana) and the Lapidarium of the Monastery of the basilica of San Paolo fuori le Mura (no. 190 Via Ostiense) – can only be viewed after submitting a written request. The Lapidarium, in fact, also contains material from the Jewish catacombs.

Returning to Piazza in Piscinula note on your left the medieval church of *San Benedetto* which, together with the church of Santa Caterina in Trastevere, appears in documents from the mid 15th to early 16th century as a point of reference for locating other synagogues and a *terrineo cum balneo nuncupato more hebreorum michovè* – that is, ritual baths (*mikveh*).

After emancipation, Jewish life in Trastevere returned to normal – and it is now the area of the city with the densest concentration of Jewish institutions. To the left of the piazza, at no. 1 Via Arco de' Tolomei, stands the striking tower building that houses the Pitigliani Jewish Centre (tel. 5800539), an ex-Jewish orphanage. Built in 1929 to replace the pre-1917 structure with more adequate facilities, the building was named after the benefactors Giuseppe and Violante Pitigliani in 1930. It now houses socio-cultural and recreational activities. The second floor is occupied by the Jewish Cultural Centre, which provides a documentation and information service for the Rome Community and is equipped with a library and teaching and audio-visual material. It is open all year round (tel. 5897589).

On the other side of Viale di Trastevere, at no. 14 Lungotevere Sanzio is the building housing the Jewish Nurseries and Nursery Schools, founded in 1874 as a result of the fusion of two confraternities: *Etz Chaim* ('Tree of Life') and *Talmud Torah* ('Study of the Torah'). The building also houses the Angelo Sacerdoti Primary School, the Rabbinical College and the Department of Cultural Assistance to the Jewish Communities of Italy. The building was reconstructed in 1962 by Giuseppe Piperno, following the demolition of the 1913 structure designed by G. B. Milani.

Next door at no. 12 is the Vittorio Polacco Primary School, built to designs by Angelo Di Castro (1956-58) and often cited as a typical example of school design of the time. It was built to replace the 1910 building (→ Itinerary I/*Spanish Temple*) which had become inadequate to deal with the sharp rise in pupils following the 1923 Gentile Reform establishing that 'the basis and culmination of elementary education is the teaching of the Christian faith'. A plaque on the facade commemorates the 112 Jewish schoolchildren murdered in Nazi concentration camps. At no. 9 are the offices of the Union of Italian Jewish Communities, UCEI (tel. 5803667), and at no. 5 is the Union's Bibliographical Centre. Opened in 1990, this centre collects and conserves all material relating to the cultural heritage of the Jewish communities of Italy (tel. 5803690). The ceiling in the conference room was painted by Emanuele Luzzati and depicts the signs of the zodiac.

At no. 60 Viale di Trastevere are the offices of the Community's Social Services, the Deputazione Ebraica di Assistenza. This association was created in 1885 as a result of the merger of the four 'social services' confraternities which during the days of the ghetto had guaranteed the survival of the poorer members of the community.

It is worth stopping to take a look at the arches and twin-columns of the Romanesque cloisters in the hospice of *San Cosimato*, now a hospital (no. 76, Via Roma Libera). On the wall to the left as you enter, among the Roman and early Christian fragments, there are some tomb inscriptions in Greek from the Monteverde catacombs (3rd-4th century CE). The first, and most legible, refers to a *Domnus*, the archon of the Vernacoli synagogue.

The *Museum of Folklore and Roman Vernacular Poetry* (1b, Piazza San Egidio) contains three paintings by Ettore Roesler Franz (1845-1907), who portrayed various aspects of ghetto life, and a drawing by Bartolomeo Pinelli (1781-1885) of *The Tournament of the Hunchback Jews* – a scene inspired by Carnival games.

Itinerary IV: the Aventine and the Caelian: Roseto di Roma, Santa Sabina, and the church of the Santi Quattro Coronati

THE ROSE GARDEN OF ROME

The springtime visitor who passes along Via del Circo Massimo and stops at the foot of the monument to Giuseppe Mazzini to admire the view of the Circus Maximus and the ruins on the Palatine cannot help but notice the swathes of roses at the foot of the Aventine. This is the *Roseto di Roma* (Rose Garden of Rome) in the area of the former Jewish cemetery – a fact commemorated by the stele bearing the Tablets of the Law at the entrance to the two fields (nos. 6 and 7 Via di Valle Murcia).

In 1587 the site of the previous Porta Portese cemetery was expropriated from the *Ghemilut Chasadim* confraternity, and a decree issued by Urban VIII ordered it to be enclosed with a wall made from the broken-up tombstone, thus ensuring the 'Jews' Yard' could not be extended further. In 1645 the confraternity obtained Innocence X's permission to acquire a cemetery site at the foot of the

The 'Rose Garden' in the area of the Jewish cemetery on the Aventine

*The Aventine Jewish cemetery in the
late 19th-century (Archivio FACE –
Centro bibliografico UCEI)*

The church of the Santi Quattro Coronati, fresco (1246) depicting the dispute between Pope Sylvester and the Roman rabbis

Church of Santa Sabina, detail of the mosaic with the ecclesia ex circumcisione

Aventine, as long as the price paid did not exceed 5,000 scudi. To render the withdrawal from the old cemetery definitive, the pope required that *Ghemilut Chasadim* level the terrain 'giving them to that end permission to take clay from the old walls and thus ruin and destroy the old city walls of Rome'. Since 1895 the Jews of Rome have not been buried at the foot of the Aventine but in the Jewish section of the Verano cemetery (→ Itinerary IX).

In 1934 the *governatorato* of Rome expropriated the Aventine site for reasons of 'public utility' in view of the construction of a new 'Triumphal' way through Rome. As with segregation inside the gates of the ghetto, the Jews of Rome complied with town planning schemes that seemed to admit no argument (the 1922 plans for the city had already envisaged the clearing of the Circus Maximus and the opening of a wide road). Nevertheless, the community asked the *governatorato* for technical assistance in removing their dead to the cemetery of Verano, and the authorities did meet the cost. In the end some 372 of the more recent tombs and funeral monuments were transferred to the new cemetery. But only four of the older tombs, discovered during the work of evacuation, were recovered and transferred to Verano. In line with the edicts issued by Urban VIII in 1625 and Pius VI in 1775 banning marking Jewish graves with tombstones, that older part of the original cemetery seems to have been made up of unnamed graves – and in all probability the earliest layer of tombs still lies undisturbed beneath the roses, thus respecting the Jewish prescription for perpetual burial.

THE CHURCH OF SANTA SABINA

Continuing down Via Santa Sabina you come to the church of the same name. This 5th-century basilica is well worth a visit, as is the rest of the hill, with its gardens, fine views, atmospheric villas and historic churches.

On the outside wall of the church portico, to the right of the entrance, there is a fragment of an inscription with Hebrew lettering, probably originally from the nearby cemetery. More interesting is a strip of mosaic to be found above the main doorway inside the basilica with a 5th-century Latin verse inscription set in gold against a blue background. Claimed to be the work of the saint Paolino da Nola, it bears the names of the founder of the church, Peter of Illyria, and Pope Celestine I. The two figures at ends of the mosaic represent, on the right, the church created by the Gentiles (*ecclesia ex gentibus*), and on the left, the church arising from Judaism, depicted with a book in Hebrew letters (*ecclesia ex circumcisione*). This is one of the oldest iconographical references to Judaism in Rome – even if Judaism is only seen as a source of Christianity. As the Middle Ages progressed, the relation between the two religions would be depicted in an ever more rigid manner, with a vast repertoire of images showing triumphal churches contrasting with blind or blindfolded synagogues.

THE CHURCH OF THE SANTI QUATTRO CORONATI

A far from mild theological dispute can be seen in the frescoes that decorate the church of the Santi Quattro Coronati ('Four Crowned Saints'), near the Coliseum on the way from the Aventine to the Caelian. Founded in the 4th century and burnt down by the Normans in 1084, the present church was rebuilt in the 12th century and contains the oratory of San Silvestro giving onto the portico between the two courtyards. The frescoes painted in 1246 document those public theological debates Jews were often summoned to take part in with the ecclesiastical authorities, who tried either to convert them or, failing that, to denigrate their religion. The episode here is also depicted in frescoes in the church of San Silvestro, Tivoli (→), painted some thirty years earlier, and is likewise recorded in Jewish sources. It forms part of the legends that surround the figure of

Pope Sylvester I and Emperor Constantine, whose conversion led to the spread of Christianity throughout the Roman Empire.

The fresco cycle starts to the left of the doorway, showing the pope baptising Constantine, and thus curing him of leprosy. The healed emperor then submits to the pontiff, and acts as squire, leading him in a triumphal procession through Rome. The frescoes on the right wall depict various miracles performed by the pope, including the theological dispute with the rabbis of Rome (shown with their traditional *tallithim* or prayer shawls) in the presence of the emperor. The episode depicted shows Rabbi Zamberi killing a bull by whispering the name of God and Sylvester bringing it back to life by uttering the name of Christ. At the end of the dispute, the rabbis and the pagan arbiters of the discussion all had to convert to Christianity. The whole episode was aimed at demonstrating the superiority of the Christian faith to Constantine, whose mother Elena, legend has it, was originally attracted by Judaism. In fact, the next fresco seems to mark the conclusion of the legend, showing the now Christian Elena finding a relic of the True Cross.

The entire fresco cycle is particularly significant, considering it was painted at a time when Italy was the scene of a clash between two ideologies: a secular conception of the Empire, personified by Frederick II, who welcomed Jewish scientists and scholars to his court and often protected the economic interests of Jewish communities, and a theocratic conception of the papacy embodied by Innocence III and Gregory IX, who insisted on the continuing validity of the donation of Constantine, and thus the temporal power of the pope. During those years the Jews in Rome were required to wear a distinguishing badge, while copies of the Talmud were confiscated and the first public burnings of Jewish books took place.

Itinerary V: Porta Capena, Roman Forum, Arch of Titus, Templum Pacis and Mamertine Prisons and the Capitol

FROM PORTA CAPENA TO THE IMPERIAL FORUM

Returning with their prisoners from victorious foreign campaigns, Roman emperors and their armies used to follow a well-established route in their triumphant re-entry into the city. Approaching along the Appian Way, they then passed through the Camene woods near Porta Capena (the present-day Piazza Capena). According to Juvenal (late 1st century CE), there was already a community of Jews in this area. Starting from the south-eastern slopes of the Palatine, our own itinerary goes first to the Imperial Forum and then continues with a visit to the Arch of Titus (entrance in Via di San Gregorio).

ARCH OF TITUS

The Arch of Titus was probably built by Domitian some time just after the death of Titus in 81 CE. In the inscription on the east side of the arch, Titus is described as *divo*, that is, a post mortem divinity. At the centre of the coffered vault Titus is shown astride an eagle, a further reference to this apotheosis. The arch itself was designed to commemorate the defeat of the Jews by Titus and his father Vespasian in 71 CE. The small frieze above the archivolt (only the central part on the east side is extant) depicts his triumph, while two other episodes in the same campaign are depicted in the large bas-relief panels on the inside walls of the arch. The south wall shows the victorious army passing through the Triumphal Arch at the beginning of the ceremony of celebration – note the men carrying booty from the Temple in Jerusalem: silver horns and a seven-branch candelabra. The placards probably originally bore the names of the conquered cities. The panel on the north wall depicts the key moment in the triumphal re-entry into Rome: preceded by lictors,

The western front of the Arch of Titus

ROME

Titus moves forwards while the goddess Rome holds the bridle of his horses and Victory crowns the emperor in his chariot. Behind come allegorical figures depicting the Roman populace (bare-chested young man) and the Roman Senate (young man in a toga).

Originally in marble, the Arch was extensively restored in 1822 by Valadier using travertine stone, as is recorded by an inscription on the side towards the Roman Forum.

The Jews of Rome always avoided passing under the Arch, and it was only in 1948 – after the proclamation of the State of Israel – that they solemnly passed beneath it, in the opposite direction from the ancient triumphal processions.

TEMPLUM PACIS AND THE MAMERTINE PRISONS

Leaving the Imperial Forum on the side of Largo Romolo e Remo, you reach the remains of the *Templum Pacis*. Built by Vespasian from 71 to 75 CE to commemorate the victory over the Jews it was destroyed by fire in 192 CE and rebuilt shortly afterwards. Following a number of earthquakes in the 5th century, the badly-damaged structure was abandoned to its fate, as the 6th-century writer Procopius relates. This building was used to house the booty brought from Jerusalem, conserved here together with numerous works of art as if in a museum. However, all trace of the contents has been lost. The temple originally occupied the end of a vast porticoed area surrounded by various buildings. Now only a few rare remains survive near the basilica of Massentius – behind the church of Santi Cosma e Damiano – and next to the Torre dei Conti in Largo Corrado Ricci.

Passing further down Via dei Fori Imperiali you come to the *Mamertine Prisons*, the medieval name for the Tullianum, a prison and site of executions in ancient Roman days. The building dates in part from the 2nd century BCE. A plaque on the wall

Funerary inscription for Gentilesca and Jo'av Croccolo from the Jewish cemetery in Trastevere (Musei Capitolini; photo Archivio Musei Capitolini)

Entrance to the Mamertine Prisons

commemorates the famous figures incarcerated and executed here, including the Jews Aristobulus II (61 BCE) and Shimon bar Ghiora (70 CE). Finally, walking up the Capitol, in Via del Tempio di Giove, you come to the remains of the *Temple of Jupiter*. After 70 CE the Jews of the city had to pay a tribute (*fiscus judaicus*) to this temple instead of the tax originally paid to the Temple of Jerusalem.

THE CAPITOL

The Capitoline Museums occupy the two buildings giving onto the Piazza del Campidoglio: the *Palazzo dei Conservatori*, on the right, and the *Palazzo Nuovo* on the left. The facades were designed by Michelangelo, initiated by Giacomo della Porta in 1563 and then completed in a second phase of work by Girolamo Rainaldi in the mid 17th century. The museums contain the largest collection of tomb inscriptions from the Trastevere cemetery (→ Itinerary III) – five capitals and one cippus – as well as a collection of inscriptions found in the Vigna Randanni catacombs. Because of restoration work, only three capitals are on display – in the Christian Monuments Room on the ground floor in the Palazzo dei Conservatori. The Hebrew inscription on top of the first capital commemorates a woman, Gentilesca, and her rabbi son, Jo'av Croccolo, who died in 1570 and 1573, respectively. The second capital bears an inscription adorned above and below with sober floral decoration; it records the burial of Shemuel Zaddiq, son of Avraham Zaddiq Ashkenazi, in 1575. The third inscription commemorates Shabbetai Cammeo, who died in 1560. The other three inscriptions (not on public display) concern Piacentina, wife of Itzhaq Panzieri (1561); Donna, daughter of Moshe Pardo and wife of Rabbi Reuven Afdon (1562); and Josef, son of Ovadia Veneziano (1572).

Palazzo Senatorio is the seat of the Rome City Council. A 1995 plaque inside the building at the end of the Galleria di Sisto IV commemorates all those Jews who worked for the City Council and were forced to give up their jobs because of the 1938 Racial Laws.

Itinerary VI: St John Lateran and Via Tasso

During the visit to the *Basilica of St John Lateran*, stop at the cloister (1215-32) – a masterpiece of Cosmati work. Amongst the various Roman and early Christian fragments placed along the walls on the left as you go in, are two Roman capitals with Hebrew funereal inscriptions from the Trastevere cemetery dedicated to Shelomo da Turano (1558) and Avraham, son of Shelomo Roccas (1587). The first inscription is in rhyming couplets above a crenellated tower – possibly the Temple of Jerusalem or a reference to the family's place of origin. The second inscription is surrounded by sober floral decoration. The marble plaque next to the doorway into the exhibition hall is more difficult to interpret. It is a fragment with a Cosmati-work cross on the left side, while the right side is divided into three panels. In the top left is a *menorah* and some Latin script; in the lower section an inscription includes the date 21 April 1574; but while the year is calculated according to the Jewish calendar (without the thousands), the day and month are calculated according to the civil calendar, despite being in Hebrew.

MUSEUM OF THE LIBERATION

The Museum of the Liberation of Rome (no. 145 Via Tasso) is in the building which in 1943-44 was a Gestapo barracks and prison. Thus there is no better place to remind Romans and visitors of the struggle for liberation during those years of Nazi torture, violence and betrayal. The museum occupies three floors and now houses a permanent exhibition of newspapers, posters and leaflets from the period of that clandestine struggle, along with precious records relating to the imprisoned and the killed found in the German police archives.

Name: *Di Porto*   Dienstgrad: *Händler* | Zelle: *356*
                          Beruf:

Vorname: *Giacomo*   Geboren am *15. 4. 90* in *Roma*

Einheit, Wohnung: *Roma, Via dei Funari 99a*
(Offene Angabe), (Ort, Strasse, Nr.)

	Einlieferung		**Entlassung**
am *24 III. 44* um *12* Uhr	Abgenommene Gegenstände:	am *24. III. 44* um Uhr	
durch *Polizei, dienste*	*Roma*	auf Grund: —	
S P D (Name, Dienstgrad)		*durch S.D.*	
(Dienststelle)		*405 Hauser*	
wegen : *Jude*		Abgeholt von : (Name, Dienstgrad)	
		(Dienststelle)	
Untersuchungshaft - Strafmaas : (Zutreffendes unterstreichen)	Vermerk über Teilrückgabe (z. B. bei Geld) auf der Rückseite.	Empfangsbescheinigung :	
Strafende :	Abgelieferte Gegenstände zurückerhalten am .... , ... Unterschrift	Unterschrift, (Wenden).	

File for a Jewish prisoner in the Gestapo prisons with the word Jude

Cloister of St John in Lateran, funerary inscription for Shelomo da Turano, from the Jewish cemetery in Trastevere, 1558

You can visit the grim cells as they were at the time, with their windows bricked up by the SS. The walls are covered with graffiti: messages, reflections, poems and phrases full of courage and hope for the liberation of Italy, written by the likes of Giuliano Vassalli, Arrigo Paladini and General Simone Simoni. Other graffiti records the capture and murder of Don Giuseppe Morosini and Bruno Buozzi, the shootings at Forte Bravetta and the massacre at La Storta.

Cell 1 contains documentation relating to the slaughter at the Fosse Ardeatine (→ Itinerary IX), where a total of 335 people (including 75 Jews) were killed in retaliation for the partisan attack in Via Rasella. Many of those killed were already held in prison by the Gestapo, and the exhibition includes their prison records. A display case on the ground floor contains fragments of rope and clothing recovered from the bodies after the massacre in the quarry was discovered.

Cell 10 is dedicated to the memory of the Jews who died at the Fosse Ardeatine or as a result of deportation. The exhibited documents include SS commander Kappler's detailed report on the deportation of sixteen Jews, and the prison records of various Jews (clearly marked with the word *Jude*). Georges de Canino's painting *The Prisoner in Via Tasso* was hung in the room next to the entrance in 1993. It was dedicated to the Jewish community on the fiftieth anniversary of the 16th October raids and, in particular, commemorates Arrigo Paladini, who wrote a first-hand account of detention in the Gestapo prisons.

Itinerary VII: the Esquiline and the Viminale: San Pietro in Vincoli, Madonna dei Monti, and the Di Castro Oratory

SAN PIETRO IN VINCOLI

As in the other centres of Italian art, numerous artists in Rome during both the Renaissance and the Baroque pe-

Church of Madonna dei Monti, facade with an inscription concerning the Catechumens

Church of San Pietro in Vincoli,
Michelangelo, Moses

Di Castro Oratory, 1914

riod chose to depict scenes and figures from the Bible. As a single example of this tendency this itinerary includes Michelangelo's statue of *Moses* in the church of *San Pietro in Vincoli* – not only for its undoubted interest as a famous work of art, but also because of the particular place it has in the hearts of visitors of all nationalities and creeds.

The church of San Pietro in Vincoli was built in the 5th century to house the chains that had manacled the saint, and was restored over the period 1471-1503 under the auspices of Cardinal Della Rovere, the future Pope Julius II, whose funeral monument is in the right transept; the present tomb is a modest-scale reduction of the grandiose tomb the pope had commissioned from Michelangelo for St Peter's. Michelangelo, in fact, worked on the project for three years, but under Julius II's successor, Leo X, he was ordered to cut back the scale of the work dramatically (the reasons for this decision, it seems, being more than simply financial) and the artist eventually came to refer to the whole affair as 'the tragedy of the tomb'. The original project envisaged a total of forty statues, including the two *Slaves* (1513-14, now in the Louvre) and the four *Prisoners* (1520-22, now in the Accademia Gallery, Florence). The crowning figure of the mausoleum is the seated figure of *Moses*, which Michelangelo began in 1514. Right from the outset Michelangelo scholars have put forward the conflicting theories as to the significance of the presence and attitude of the Jewish leader. Most agree, however, that the artist has depicted a worried Moses indignantly witnessing the scenes of idolatry the Jews indulged in while he had been on Mount Sinai.

A very original and interesting interpretation of the statue was put forward by Sigmund Freud, who studied it during his 1913 visit to Rome: 'Michelangelo has placed on the pope's mausoleum a new Moses, a figure that goes beyond the traditional, historical Moses. In designing the shattered tablets of the Law the focus is not on Moses' destructive anger but rather on his calming his rage... or at least the restraint preceding action. As a result, he has imbued the figure of Moses with something new – something superhuman. The formidable muscled mass of the figure becomes the physical means for the expression of man's highest endeavour: the controlling of passion for the sake of a cause to which one is devoted.'

In the niches to the sides, the statues of *Lea* and *Rachel* symbolise the active and contemplative life respectively. Designed by Michelangelo, they were executed by Raffaello da Montelupo (all the other parts of the mausoleum are also the work of his assistants).

In the crypt under the main altar of the church there is an early-Christian sarcophagus. Legend has it that this contains the bodies of the seven brothers who, during the Maccabees' uprising against Antiochus Epiphanes (175-164 BCE), refused to deny their religion and were killed by the Syrian conqueror. The episode is related in both the second book of the Maccabees and in the Talmud.

CHURCH OF THE MADONNA
DEI MONTI

At the end of Via Madonna dei Monti stands the church giving the street its name. Designed by Giacomo della Porta, it was designated a *Catechumenorum familia* in 1580 by Gregory XIII, as the inscription on the facade tells us. The church marks a turning-point in the papal policy with regard to the conversion of *Hebrei et Infideli*. This change began with the preaching of Ignatius Loyola and the work of his Opera, later to become the Arch-Confraternity running the 'holy places for Catechumens and Neophytes', offering teaching of Christian doctrine and assistance to new converts.

Since 1543, under Pope Paul III, these roles had been played by the churches of San Giovanni in

Mercatello and San Venanzio al Campidoglio, and in 1562 a Nunnery for Converted Women was set up, soon followed by a *collegio* for male neophytes and a *conservatorio* for women neophytes. All of these institutions were financed by a tribute of ten gold ducats imposed on all the synagogues in the Papal States. With the appointment of Cardinal Guglielmo Sirleto as 'judge ordinary of neophytes and catechumens' (in the words of the facade inscription), the work of conversion began to be centred on the church of Madonna dei Monti.

In 1634 Urban VIII had the building next to the church and convent constructed. This can still be seen at the corner of Via dei Neofiti, and – according to the inscription on the facade – used to house the *Hospitio Cathecumenoru*m, hospice for catechumens. Dedicated to San Silvestro and San Pantaleone, it underwent restoration in 1762. Jews of all ages were brought here – often against their will (on the basis of false testimony or extorted consent) – and only rarely were the protests of the ghetto able to obtain their release.

Jews were strictly forbidden to come anywhere near these streets, and an edict of 1635 laid down severe penalties for those who disobeyed: 'let no Catechumen or Neophyte, even if long since a member of the Holy Faith… dare or presume under any cause, pretext or enquiry whatsoever, trade, negotiate, converse or engage in business, either for his own interests or by means of other persons, with Jews and Infidels.'

THE DI CASTRO ORATORY

The Di Castro Oratory (no. 33 Via Cesare Balbo) was built in 1914, just ten years after the opening of the Temple, thanks to the munificence of Grazia Pontecorvo, the widow of Salvatore Di Castro. The oratory met a need felt by quite a few Jewish families, who after the emancipation of the ghetto had gone to live in other residential areas of the city far from the Temple on the Lungotevere. Temporary measures, such as the oratory set up in an apartment in Via Modena, had proved to be inadequate. The square room has a single central women's gallery: the position of the *aron* and *tevah*, together with the sober decoration of the walls and ceiling, are typical of the style of post-emancipation synagogues. The candelabra on the *tevah* and the lamps (*ner tamid*) in front of the *aron* came from the Scola Castigliana. The stained-glass windows (1991) are the work of Aldo Di Castro. Since 1972 the basement rooms of the oratory have housed the Ashkenazi temple. Designed by Angelo Di Castro, this synagogue follows the rite that originated with the Jews from Central and Eastern Europe. The 18th-century gilded wood doors of the *aron* and the candelabra again come from the Scola Castigliana.

Itinerary VIII: Museum of Rome, Vatican Museums and National Roman Museum

Housed in Palazzo Braschi (no. 10 Piazza San Pantaleo), the Museum of Rome has a collection of paintings and sculptures reflecting the history of the city, including nine atmospheric watercolours by Ettore Roesler Franz (1845-1907) depicting the most characteristic corners of the ghetto – Portico of Ottavia, Via Rua, Piazza delle Azzimelle and Vicolo Capocciuto – in the series 'The Rome That Is No More'.

In the City Print Cabinet on the top floor you can, on request, view the three 1823 engravings by Bartolomeo Pinelli depicting an attack on the ghetto and a Jew being rolled in a barrel by the mob. These works are part of the illustrations for a burlesque poem *Meo Patacca ovvero Roma in feste nei trionfi di Vienna* ('Meo Patacca, or Rome in celebration over the triumphs of Vienna') written in 1695 by Giuseppe Berneri after the defeat of the Turks at the gates of Vienna. The work recounts, in language liberally scattered with expressions from the Jewish-Roman vernacular,

B. Pinelli, Meo Patacca calms down the
crowd trying to set fire to the ghetto,
1823 (Gabinetto comunale delle stampe)

Funerary plaque for Primitiva
and Eufrenon from the Catacombs
of Monteverde (Musei Vaticani;
photo by the Archivio Musei Vaticani)

Sarcophagus with the spirits of
the seasons and menorah
(Museo Nazionale Romano,
photo by Archivio Musei Vaticani)

how the Roman people rose to the Jews' defence and quelled a nascent pogrom in the city.

In the same building the City Photographic Archives contain material relating to the demolition and rebuilding work carried out at the turn of the century, with more than 150 photographs of the ghetto and the old *scole*.

THE VATICAN MUSEUMS

The Vatican Museums (Viale Vaticano) contain the largest collection of Hebrew inscriptions from the Jewish catacombs (visits upon written request). There are almost 200 on display in one special room (access via the Museo Pio Cristiano or the Museo Gregoriano). Most come from the Monteverde catacomb, the first to be discovered and explored (by Bosio in 1602). Many of the inscriptions are decorated with illustrations of the ritual furnishings from the ruined Temple of Jerusalem, which had by then become veritable symbols of the Jewish faith: the small plaque dedicated to *ACTHP* (Aster) is decorated with a *menorah* flanked by two pecking birds, an image also commonly found in Christian iconography.

On another plaque the text is flanked by a *menorah* and an open *aron*. The dedicatee, Gaudenzia, is described in Greek as a priestess; presumably this title refers to the fact she was the wife (or daughter) of a Coen. But she may well also have had a definite liturgical role. One of the most problematic – and hence interesting – inscriptions is an Aramaic text, which may be read as follows: 'Annias, son-in-law of Bar-Calabria'.

Among the objects on display note an oil lamp decorated with an image of a *menorah*, probably made in North Africa in the 3rd century CE.

The display cases in the Apostolic Library contain examples of 'golden glassware' – the bottom of glass beakers decorated with gold leaf between two layers of glass. These were placed next to, or within, the opening to catacomb loculi, perhaps to facilitate

Gilded glass (Biblioteca Apostolica Vaticana; photo by Archivio Biblioteca Apostolica Vaticana)

identification of the tomb. Only eleven of those discovered so far are clearly Jewish in character. These show the *menorah* and open *aron* flanked by lions, or the more unusual arrangement of a building within a colonnaded piazza, with, below, a *menorah*, an *etrog* and a *lulav*. Unfortunately in a very poor condition, this piece has been interpreted as a representation of the Temple of Jerusalem.

NATIONAL ROMAN MUSEUM

The most famous Jewish artefact in the National Roman Museum (no. 67 Piazzale Cinquecento; presently being restored) is the broken front of a 3rd-century marble sarcophagus with, in the middle, a *menorah* behind the figure of Victory holding a clipeus. The decoration of the side panels consists of allegories of the Seasons, a recurrent motif in Classical art. Clearly the front panel was only half-finished when it was acquired by a Jewish patron who had the *menorah* carved in the space that was usually reserved for a portrait of the deceased.

The museum also contains material from the Roman catacombs (forty or so lamps, loculi plaques and sarcophagi) and a single (unfortunately incomplete) 2nd-century tombstone found at Castel Porziano and once on the tomb acquired by the Jerusiarch Caius Julius Justus for himself and his family on land paid for by funds collected amongst the Jewish community. The collection was instigated by a *pater synagogae* (Livius Dionysius), a Jerusiarch (name unknown) and a life *Antonius* (*dia biu*). The site of the find is presumably further evidence for the presence of a Jewish community in nearby Ostia (→).

The museum also contains a fragment of a silver plaque engraved on one side with a representation of flowers in a vase decorated with a bean motif, and on the other with the text of a liturgical blessing including the names of angels (some were claimed to watch over new-born children and their mothers). Beneath this text is engraved the name of a child – Yosef,

Verano cemetery,
the tomb of Samuele Alatri

Verano cemetery,
the Pincetto funerary monuments

Villa Torlonia catacombs,
detail of a painted cubicle (photo by
Archivio Centro di cultura ebraica)

son of Yehuda – confirming that this 17th-18th-century piece was a protective amulet to be hung on a child's crib.

Itinerary IX: Outside the walls of Rome: the Verano cemetery, the catacombs of Villa Torlonia and Vigna Randanini, the Appian Way and the Fosse Ardeatine

The *Verano cemetery*, or Campo Verano, contains a Jewish section that was first opened in January 1895, as is recorded by a plaque just inside the entrance gateway bearing the inscription 'Cemeterio Israelitico'.

In 1916 the Community acquired an adjoining plot of land from the City Council, thus guaranteeing for the first time that its dead could receive perpetual burial. Visitors enter the cemetery by the small entrance to the side of the main gateway in Via Tiburtina. The main avenue leads up to the small temple in which the rites for the dead are celebrated. In front of the temple is Angelo Di Castro's cippus commemorating the Roman Jews deported by the Nazis, unveiled on 16 October 1952.

The portico to the funeral chapel contains some 17th-18th-century plaques describing funeral rites and dispositions. Behind the building stands the monument to the Jews who died in Libya, designed by Eddy Levy and Massimiliano Beltrame (1977). Passing down the avenue, the area on the left contains the oldest tombs; those nearest the perimeter wall are the tombs brought here from the Aventine cemetery in 1934 (→ Itinerary IV/*Roseto di Roma*). The Roman Jews refer to this area as 'Il Pincetto' – that is, the 'small Pincio'. Here you can see family tombs and graves dating from the beginning of the 20th century. Their style and decoration echo the eclectic taste of the recently-built Temple, and at times they even echo the architectural features of the new synagogue. If you enter the Verano cemetery by the San Lorenzo

Villa Torlonia catacombs, detail of a dolphin on a trident (photo by Archivio Centro di cultura ebraica)

entrance, directly opposite you – at the end of the main avenue – is the Monument to the Deported, commemorating the 2,728 Romans who died in the Nazi concentration and death camps.

THE VILLA TORLONIA AND
VIGNA RANDANINI CATACOMBS
AND THE APPIAN WAY

The catacombs were the Jewish burial grounds in ancient Rome. Five have survived. From north to south, they are at Villa Torlonia in Via Nomentana, Vigna Apolloni in Via Labicana, Vigna Cimarra and Vigna Randanini in Via Appia, and Monteverde in Via Portuense. Only two are open to visitors: Villa Torlonia and Vigna Randanini. For years the catacombs were under the supervision of the Pontifical Commission for the Archaeology of Sacred Sites, but then in 1984 they were entrusted to the Archaeology Department of Rome City Council (tel. 4882364 to book a visit; take a torch).

The entrance to the *Villa Torlonia catacombs* is in the garden of the villa (entrance in Via Spallanzani). The last to be discovered (in 1918), this site in fact consists of two separate burial areas of different dates subsequently united. The tunnels run for almost one kilometre and cover more than 13,000 square metres. Access is by what was the western entrance to the oldest part of the catacombs, dating from the beginning of the 3rd century and extended until the beginning of the following century. The slightly apse-shaped space is uncovered, possibly due to the need to stand round the coffin before actual burial. The area to the right of the entrance has two main characteristics: regularly-placed loculi laid out between pilaster strips carved into the tufa, and the presence of the slightly bigger *arcosolium loculi* framed by a very low arch. These were used as double tombs, with tiled partitions. In the area to the left the wall is divided in a different way, with simple plaster lines

Vigna Randanini catacombs, a cubicle vault decorated with a painting of Fortune *(photo by Archivio Centro di cultura ebraica)*

Vigna Randanini catacombs, walls and vault painted with menorahs (photo by Archivio Centro di cultura ebraica)

Vigna Randanini catacombs, detail of the 'Palm' cubicle (photo by Archivio Centro di cultura ebraica)

delineating regular spaces for the loculi. Going back to the central tunnel you pass over a pre-existing drain, and moving further down the tunnel you come to the eastern area of the catacombs, where there are painted loculi. The designs are all rather similar, with the *menorah* at the centre of the vault flanked by dolphins with tridents and/or plant motifs delimiting a space containing cintrons (*etrog*) and horns (*shofar*). Note in particular the inside of the *arcosolium loculi* decorated with an open *aron* (with the Scrolls of the Law). Above it are the sun and moon and to the sides two candelabra, an amphora of oil, a horn, citron and other features alluding to the ruined Temple of Jerusalem.

In ancient times the main entrance to the *Vigna Randanini catacombs* was reached by a small road leading from the Appian Way. That original entrance is now on private property, so the present entrance is an open-air space in Via Appia Pignatelli. When discovered in 1859, this space was believed to be a synagogue. It is actually a reconverted pre-existing room used for funerary purposes. The surviving parts of the original space dating from 1st century BCE to 1st century CE, are the two apses in tufa and brick trellis-work and the mosaic niche.

The *arcosolium loculi* in the side and end walls, specially built for the purpose, date from a later period, and are characterised by the use of alternate bands of brickwork and tufa, typical of the 4th century. The floor in black and white mosaic may date from the same period.

As you enter there are no tombs in the first space, nor in the tunnel to the right. They are now mainly used to store marble fragments and loose plaques. In fact, none of the almost 200 loculi plaques found inside the catacombs was in place, a sure sign that they had been thoroughly looted by grave robbers.

The inscriptions are mainly in Greek. But there are also some in

Appian Way, plaque with names of freed slaves

Latin, and others in a combination of languages and scripts. There is no trace of Hebrew.

The first gallery that opens up a few metres further on contains a series of cubicles used for multiple tombs. In the second cubicle, with a plastered rear, there is a painting of a *menorah*. The ceiling, too, is decorated with a fruit motif (perhaps citron). Further on there are individual loculi, before you come to the 'oven' tombs. Known in Hebrew as *kokhim*, these tombs are dug at ground level perpendicular to the tunnel wall. This form of tomb is typical of the Middle East and North Africa and is totally absent in all the other catacombs in Rome (Jewish or otherwise). It was thus a special feature of Judaism in ancient Rome.

A little further on is the so-called 'palm' cubicle, so named because of the four palm trees decorating its corners. The lower part of the sides are decorated with painted marble panels, while in the upper parts are still visible a vase of water and roses. The base of the vault and the original *arcosolia* are outlined in red. This tomb was re-used, with extra loculi being added in the side walls and above the vault. Unfortunately these additions ruined the original decoration.

Another painted cubicle can be seen in the innermost part of the catacomb. The walls and vault of this double-chambered tomb are richly decorated in the 'linear' style, with red and green lines defining geometric spaces containing naturalistic and mythological representations. The main decoration is to be seen on the keystones of the vault: one shows Victory crowning a naked young man, the second shows the figure of Fortune with a cornucopia.

The various panels are decorated with real and mythological animals (peacock, hen, fish, and hippocampus), plant motifs, cherubs and even a sheep with a winged-staff, an allusion to Mercury. Such paintings can also be found in Christian Roman catacombs and can be dated to around the second half of the 2nd century. Both of these cubicles pre-date the Jewish catacombs and were incorporated some time later. They had separate entrances, and were probably not in use when the Jews began to bury their dead here.

Scholars have long discussed the Jewish prohibition on the representation of the human figure; but as is shown by the paintings in the Dura Europos synagogue in Syria (first half of the 3rd century) and the mosaics in the Galilee synagogues (5th-6th century), this proscription was not always obeyed. Clearly, in 3rd- to 4th-century Rome, when these catacombs were made, the orthodox community did not reject these pagan 'contaminations'.

On the walls are inscriptions originally located either directly over the opening of the loculi or right next to them. Engraved or painted on marble plaques, these inscriptions are not particularly accurate. The standard text reads 'here lies … may he sleep in peace.' Alongside the name there may be a reference to the youth of the deceased ('the child…') or the name of the dedicatee (usually the husband or wife) or the position (honorary or otherwise) that the deceased held in the community. Thus, for example, there are numerous *grammateos* (scribes), *archon* (head of the community) and even *arch-synagogue* (perhaps head rabbi). Unfortunately, the role or function of these figures cannot be defined with any precision.

Do not leave the Appian Way without seeing the small plaque with *menorah* once inside the Vigna Randanini catacombs and now on the outside wall of the building at no. 36A (next to the petrol station), or the plaque at 288A with the names of three, presumably Jewish, freed slaves, 'Baricha, Zabda and Achiba', who were given their freedom in the 1st century BCE by Lucius Valerius.

THE FOSSE ARDEATINE
In Via Ardeatine, about one kilometre beyond the junction with Via delle

Fosse Ardeatine, Sacrarium interior

Fosse Ardeatine,
F. Coccia, The Martyrs, *1950*

Sette Chiese, are the Fosse Ardeatine, a place that captures all the horrors of the Nazi occupation of Rome.

Here, on the evening of 24 March 1944, the SS commanded by Herbert Kappler brutally murdered 335 people, mainly civilians, in reprisal for a partisan attack in Via Rasella, in which 32 German soldiers had died. None of the victims (one was a fifteen-year-old boy) had anything to do with the partisan attack. Rounded up with the collaboration of the Rome Police authorities, they included prisoners from the Regina Coeli prison and from the Gestapo prison in Via Tasso (→ Itinerary VI) – chosen for political or 'racial' reasons – as well as hostages the Germans had seized in Via Rasella. The total included some 75 Jews, and exceeded by five the number of victims ordered (ten Italians for every German; at his trial held in 1948-53 Kappler pointed out that a wounded German soldier had died in the meantime).

The victims were shot in the back of the head, five at a time, and the Germans tried to hide the massacre by setting off mines to bring down the walls of the pozzolana quarry. Only after the liberation of Rome was it possible (thanks to the testimony of some who lived in the area) to re-construct what had happened and recover the bodies.

The forecourt to the quarry is approached through a bronze fretwork gate of thorns – the work of Mirko Basaldella, who also made the grating in the quarry monument. The statue group to the left is by Francesco Coccia (1950) and represents *The Martyrs*: the artisan, the intellectual and the adolescent, all tied by the wrist. On the high tufa wall of the quarry are the plaques commemorating the martyrs of Italy and the Resistance Gold Medals. Above, the Cross and the Star of David stand out against the sky.

To the right is the entrance to the narrow passageways leading to where the massacre was actually carried out: the gaping holes in the passageways through which light filters were a side effect of the mines the SS exploded to block the entrance. A plaque inside records the patient and difficult work of Attilio Ascarelli, professor of forensic medicine at Rome University, who had the thankless task of examining the bodies and helping the families to identify them. The passage to the left leads to the Memorial Chapel, also accessed from the open space in front of the quarry. Built in 1949 to designs by Aprile, Calcaprina, Cardelli, Fiorentino and Perugini, it is a block of reinforced concrete resting on six pillars – a single large tombstone with an overwhelming sense of oppression; underneath, in the penumbra, the tombs of the victims are all aligned in the same way.

Sacrofano

Inhabitants 3,100
Altitude 260 m
Province of Rome
Itinerary 1

Situated on Monte Musino, this village was called *Scrofano* until 1928, when it was given its current name of Sacrofano ('sacred temple'). Enclosed by two gates, the small historic centre includes the medieval church of *San Giovanni Battista*, rebuilt in the 17th century, though the bell tower is original. Just outside the village are the 18th-century *Palazzo Comunale* and the contemporary church of *San Biagio*, whose interior has frescoes.

A 16th-century cadastre records the presence of two Jews who owned small farms, bordering with the garden of the hospital near Laconcia. Other Jewish names were registered in the factor's account book. Sacrofano was one of the localities in Lazio, where Jechiel Manoscrivi carried out a circumcision (1575). In the old part of the village, near the church of San Giovanni Battista, there is still *Via Vecchio Ghetto*.

In the environs, the areas of **Bracciano**, **Campagnano**, and **Civita Castellana** had small Jewish communities from the mid-19th century. At the time of Pope Sistus v a number of Jews returned to live at **Formello**, a village at the gates of Rome, after paying an initial 20 giuli and then 12 giuli per year. The whereabouts of their houses is not known.

Sacrofano, Via del Vecchio Ghetto

Segni

Inhabitants 8,500
Altitude 668 m
Province of Rome
Itinerary 1

Nestling at the foot of the Lepini hills, and surrounded by chestnut woods, Segni takes its name from the Volscian *Signia*, possibly derived from the Sicani, an ancient people who were in Lazio before settling in Sicily. Today Segni is mainly a holiday resort.

Our visit to the historic centre begins from Porta Maggiore with its fine views of the massive polygonal town walls (once two kilometres long) and some inner town walls (at times double width). After going past the gate and some way up Via San Vitaliano, you come to Via Dante and the *Palazzo Cremona* with its late-Renaissance loggia. Returning to Via San Vitaliano you can visit the Romanesque *Duomo* (the interior is rich in 17th- and 18th-century decorations and modern statues). By following a part of the historic walls, you climb up to the upper part of Segni as far as the *Porta Saracena*, the most famous local landmark, and then on to the top of the hills, where there is an *Acropolis* (40 x 25 meters) and some interesting Roman remains.

By taking Via Santa Lucia you finally enter the medieval quarter with its well-preserved streets, passageways and courtyards. The first church is the Romanesque *Santo Stefano*. Not far away is *Via della Giudea*, where the Jews lived in the 16th century. From Via Cremona you reach the remains of the Porta in Lucino, a similar gate to the Porta Saracena. Beyond this gate is Via Umberto which

Segni

runs along stretches of the ancient walls and takes you back, after the Baroque church of *Gesu*, to Via San Vitaliano.

At Segni, every August the *Giostra del maialetto* ('pig tournament') ends with an historic pageant, while in October the *Sagra delle castagne* ('chestnut fair') is held.

In late 1555 four Jews were put on trial – Helia de Ventura from Fondi, a resident at Segni, Santoro Maymon, his brother Moises Agnetti, and Habraham, a physician from Paliano – for failing to respect the bull of Paul IV, *Cum nimis absurdum*, which forced all Jews residing in the Papal States to go and live in the ghetto.

The lack of any particularly Jewish elements of architecture in the urban fabric means the Jewish buildings cannot be identified. Thus, here more than in other cases, place names become important in locating Jewish buildings. In the historic centre, to the left on looking at the church of Santo Stefano, there is a Via della Giudea, once called Via delle Streghe. The synagogue was probably also in this street. And in 1569 it had to pay 10 scudi to the House of Catechumens in Rome. In 1578, Isias, the son of Giuseppe, a resident in Rome, was granted a licence to open a loan-bank at Segni.

JEWISH SURNAMES

In the mid-16th century Jews from many towns throughout Lazio and other regions in the Papal States came to live in the Roman ghetto, set up 15 years earlier, thus swelling its population considerably. There were many families of Jews with the same name among those who crowded into the narrow space of the *serraglio* – as the ghetto was called. The traditional names were the recurrent – Abramo, Mose, Isacco, Rubino, Ricca, Ester, Dolce, etc. – and not even the Hebrew usage of indicating the father's name was enough for a person to be univocally identified. The Roman tradition of using nicknames (and some

Segni, Via della Giudea, once called Via delle Streghe ('Witches Street')

became surnames) was of some help but still did not solve the problem. Thus it was only logical to add the name of the town of origin to distinguish one Abramo, son of Aronne, from another. As late as the 17th century we find documents with traditional surnames that survive today: Di Nepi, Di Cave, Dell'Ariccia, Di Cori, Sermoneta, Alatri, Frascati and so on. Over the centuries they lost their original meaning of provenance (i.e. *di* – 'from' Nepi, Cave or Ariccia) as they were transformed into modern family surnames. Such names provide a clue to the origins of many Roman Jews who came to live alongside those with older names such as Levi, Coen, Anav and Piattelli, whose origin goes much further back in time.

The curious cases of the Milano and Toscano families require further explanation. Their surnames derived from appointments as tax collectors for Milan or Tuscany, and not their provenance, since the Milano family originally came from Sicily, while the Toscano were a branch of the Di Segni family.

Sermoneta

Inhabitants 1,500
Altitude 257 m
Province of Latina
Itinerary 2

Situated on a ridge dominating the Pontine plain, the ancient town was called *Sulmonetum*, derived from Sulmo, meaning 'abundant water'. Traditionally a rural market town, today Sermoneta is also a tourist attraction.

Our visit to the historic centre begins in Corso Garibaldi, lined with low medieval palaces, and the 14th-century church of *San Giuseppe*. We then proceed to Piazza del Popolo, and the 16th-century *House of Girolamo Siciolante*, birthplace of the celebrated painter (1520-80). Via Santa Maria leads to the 13th-century cathedral of the *Assunta*, built over an ancient temple dedicated to Cybele, but altered several times. We then go on to the Piazza del Comune and Via della Valle with the former *Palazzo Comunale* bearing the crests of the Caetani family. From Via della Scaletta a series of steps leads up to Via della Fortezza and the 15th-century *Castello Caetani*. The well-preserved castle has a keep, bulwarks, military barracks and cisterns. Below is the small medieval quarter.

By going up a stairway you reach Piazza degli Olmi and the bulwark known as the *Cittadella*. Inside is a tall keep, the dungeons, and, in one wing, the *Casa del Cardinale* (House of the Cardinal) where Duke Valentino and the guests lodged. From the embattlements there are views as far as the Circeo headland and the sea.

*Sermoneta, Loggia dei Mercanti
('merchants') at the beginning
of the Idoli district, also called
the district of 'the Jews'*

In 1297 the people of Sermoneta swore allegiance to the Caetani, the new rulers of the town. Among those who promised their loyalty was a certain Sabatuccio Giudeo. We do not know, however, whether he represented only his family or a larger group. The first more detailed information about the Sermoneta Jewish community dates from the 15th century, when notarial deeds attest to a long-standing presence and good relations with the Christian population. A large group of around 20 families owned land and houses, furnishings and precious fabrics. Although there does not seem to have been a proper bank, they engaged in moneylending, in addition to trading with neighbouring towns, and at times even with Rome. As many as ten companies were formed by Jews and Christians – proof of the easy-going relations between the peoples of different religions. In 1423 the cathedral of Santa Maria in Sermoneta even granted three Jewish brothers a lease on a vineyard.

There is a 15th-century Hebrew manuscript in the Biblioteca Apostolica Vaticana (ms. Vat. hebr, 364) containing medical treatises by Mateus Zarfati, translated by Haim di Messer Vital 'here at Sermoneta'.

At the end of the 15th century, the short-lived rule by the Borgia family brought the first restrictive laws against the Jews. The situation, however, does not seem to have deteriorated, since the Jews in Sermoneta still viewed favourably the Borgia and even the Caetani, who when they later returned to power were less inclined to their earlier more benevolent attitude.

From the 16th century, with the Caetani back in power, there are many sales contracts concerning Jewish land and houses, suggesting the beginning of the exodus that was to be complete in 1569, when all Jews in the Papal States were enclosed in the ghettos of Rome and Ancona.

There does not seem to have been a genuine Jewish quarter in Sermoneta. But there was a spontaneous if

Sermoneta, the monkey carved on the building in the Idoli district indicated by local tradition as the 'rabbi's house'

Sermoneta, Via della Portella, near Porta Annibaldi

Sermoneta, the 'house of the monkey' in the Idoli district, seen from the Loggia dei Mercanti

Sermoneta, the tower house in Via Marconi traditionally believed to have been the synagogue

not random concentration of Jewish families in the houses (often with Christian neighbours) in the Decarcia Portella, in the Contrada degli Iodoli, also known as the Contrada delli Iudei ('Quarter of the Jews'). In the same area there was a building traditionally thought to have been the old synagogue: an elegant three storey tower-house dating from the 13th-14th century, with a double-light window at the centre of the facade on the former Via delle Scuole, later Via degli Ebrei, now Via Marconi. According to local tradition the 'rabbi's house' with the emblem of a monkey, was at the beginning of the Contrada degli Idoli.

Archive documents mention a Jewish cemetery which, according to an old cadastre, was a plot along the road to Valvisciolo at Ponte della Tomba, called Tomba delli Iudei ('Tomb of the Jews').

The surname Sermoneta is a particularly common surname for Roman Jews (→ Segni/Jewish Surnames).

THE JEWISH OATH

At the bottom of a small parchment manuscript of the notary Pietro del Giudice containing the statutes granted by the Annibaldi (the first *signori* in the area) to the town of Sermoneta and confirmed by the Caetani in 1304, a special oath was added in the 15th century to be pronounced by Sermoneta Jews before testifying in a trial.

The long formula is full of biblical references ('do you swear by ... the God who appeared to Moses at the Red Sea') and threats in case of perjury ('the earth will swallow you up as it did Dathan and Abiram'). Some of these threats are rather unusual even compared to similar documents in neighbouring areas such as, 'If you have sworn false witness then be done to you what Judith did to Holofernes'.

The oath was written in a very colourful medieval Italian vernacular with mixed dialect influences and Hebrew words in Latin letters.

Sezze

Inhabitants 8,000
Altitude 319 m
Province of Latina
Itinerary 2

Situated on a hill in the Lepini foothills, the ancient settlement of *Setia* was, according to legend, founded by Hercules. The name derives from the word *setole* – supposedly the bristles of the Nemean lion. Today an agricultural and preserve centre, the modern town has mainly developed round the railway station of Sezze Scalo.

Our visit to the town, which still has the remains of Roman walls, begins at the Porta Pascibella, Porta Sant'Andrea and the promenade of the Capuchins. Beyond these gates the promenade leads to the Capuchin church surrounded by oak woods. On the other side of the woods is Via Marconi, the street where the synagogue was situated in the 16th century.

Continuing along Via Piagge Marine takes you to the *Teatro Italiano,* a natural amphitheatre, where every Holy Friday the Passion of Christ was performed. This historic religious drama is now re-enacted as a procession through the streets of the town, attracting a large number of tourists. After going back along Via Marconi and visiting the medieval church of *San Parasceve* you come to Via Corradini and Via Cavour with large stretches of well-preserved *Roman Walls.* Opposite is the imposing 18th-century *Convent of the Poor Clares* (*Clarisse*) and an annexed Baroque church. In Largo Buozzi the *Antiquarium Comunale* (antique museum) is housed in the former Palaz-

Sezze, Via dei Chiavari

165

zo della Pretura. By returning to Via Corradini you can visit the cathedral of *Santa Maria*. Begun in the Romanesque period but consecrated in 1364, the unusual feature of the cathedral is its orientation. The original facade was demolished in 1594 and partially rebuilt at the rear. Inside, there are interesting frescoes, canvas paintings and wooden statues.

In the 15th century many names and references to Jews in the area began to appear in local documents. A manuscript of 1482 mentions Eliezhar, son of Josef ha-Lewi ha-sefardi (the 'Spaniard'), who was owed money by the Shabbethai brothers and a certain Daniele.

The town statutes mention Jews in Chapter 59, Book III, in connection with the punishments for those practising usury.

The Jewish community was recorded in the tax registers of the treasurers appointed by the Apostolic Chamber from 1472 on. Its exact whereabouts is not known, however. Some sources claim that the settlement was situated in the present Via dei Chiavari, and the synagogue (nothing has survived) must have been in Via Marconi. From an act promulgated some time after 1568, we learn that the Sezze Jews were obliged to pay 30 gold ducats for the synagogue of Piperno, by then abandoned.

The Jews returned to Sezze after 1870. A census carried out the following year recorded nine Jews out of the total population of 9,440 inhabitants. Further proof of this return is provided by the town cemetery outside the town at Zoccolanti. A small section of the graveyard was given over to Jewish graves and is separated by a wall with a gate from the Christian section.

Not far from Sezze, a small Jewish presence was recorded in **Maenza** in 1472, where one Jewish household was taxed.

Tarquinia

Inhabitants 13,500
Altitude 133 m
Province of Viterbo
Itinerary 3

Nestling on a hill near the Via Aurelia, this town has changed name several times over the centuries: from the original Etruscan *Tarxuna*, (named after Traconte who according to legend founded the settlement), to Corneto until 1872, then Corneto Tarquinia until 1922 and finally simply Tarquinia. A market town, Tarquinia now also exercises a strong tourist appeal thanks to the fame of its medieval monuments. In fact there are impressive medieval towers scattered throughout the town (eighteen are intact, while the bases of a further twenty may be seen) and town walls (3.2 kilometres long), while just outside the town you can visit the Etruscan necropolis.

The main streets lead off from the central Piazza Cavour with its Gothic-Renaissance *Palazzo Vitelleschi* built for Cardinal Giovanni Vitelleschi in the mid 15th century. Today it houses the *Tarquinia National Museum*, one of the major Italian collections of Etruscan antiquities.

From Piazza Cavour, Via Valverde goes along the walls to the Romanesque church of *Santa Maria di Valverde*, remodelled several times before the last major restoration in the mid 19th century after damage caused by tremors.

Back in Piazza Cavour, by taking Via Mazzini you reach the Piazza Duomo and the cathedral of *Santa Margherita*. Destroyed by fire and rebuilt in the mid 17th century, it has a cycle of 16th-century frescoes. Behind the cathedral, by continuing up Via Porta Castello, you come to one of the city gates. Beyond this gate is the Romanesque church of *Santa Maria di Castello* with its sumptuous interior.

Leaving Piazza Cavour by Via Roma and going as far as Piazza San Giovanni you can visit the 15th-century church of *San Giovanni Gerosolimitano* (fine frescos inside) and by crossing a number of streets you reach Via Umberto I, closed at the bottom by the Porta Romana. Just before the end of the street is the church of *Santa Lucia* with important paintings attributed to Guido Reni (1575-1642).

After returning to Piazza Cavour, you take the busy Corso Vittorio Emanuele II to reach the stage-like Piazza Matteotti. At the centre is a *Baroque fountain*, while on the sides are church of the *Suffragio* and the Romanesque *Palazzo Comunale* (remodelled several times until the 18th century). Behind this palace is the beginning of Via Antica (with an imposing tower) leading to Via San Pancrazio and the former 13th-century church with alongside the *Palazzo dei Priori* made up of four towers. By continuing along Via delle Torri past *Torre dei Draghi,* you come to Piazza Santo Stefano and *Torre Barucci* as well as several other converted towers. By making your way through various streets, you eventually come to the church of *San Martino* dominated by a majestic tower.

Having crossed the nearby Piazza della Tribuna, Via dell'Orfanotrofio and Via Marcantonio Barbarico, you reach the Romanesque church of the *Santissima Annunziata* with its ornate Sicilian-Norman portal. Having returned to Piazza Matteotti and taken Via Porta Tarquinia, flanked by medieval houses, you come to the 18th-century *Palazzo Scotti* and the Gothic-Romanesque church of *San Francesco* with its tall 16th-century bell tower.

Tarquinia, the unusual ornamental motifs similar to Jewish candelabras in the church of Santa Maria in Castello (12th century)

According to tax registers – the most accurate source for ascertaining the presence of individuals or groups – Jews from Rome lived in Tarquinia from the early decades of the 14th century.

Roman-origin families of moneylenders stayed in the town for generations: from 1293 various documents record the financial connections between the town authorities and the Jews. The recurrent names were Sabato di Gennatano, Sabato di Vitale and later Vitale di Daniele and Zaccaria. In the second half of the 14th century, as in other Tuscia settlements, many new families of Roman Jews arrived. They were attracted by the extraordinary economic growth in the region at a time when Rome was going through a difficult period of economic stagnation, partly due to the exile of the pope.

The Corneto Jews not only practised moneylending. In 1470 a manufacturer of saddlepacks, Abramo, paid the large sum of 20 ducats in tax, compared to the average of around 2 ducats. Overall the Jews were prosperous and active in various sectors. Highly resourceful, they even expanded to other areas in the province. By the early 15th century some Jews from Corneto were also active in localities, such as Acquapendente where, in 1422, there was a branch of the bank of Dattolo di Angelo from Corneto, managed by an employee, while the owner had moved to Cortona.

Due to the continuing local economic growth, the Jews' initial activity in the area continued to be moneylending. Tarquinia had become of strategic importance for the food supplies for Rome and for the easy access to ports on the coast. In addition to moneylending, Jews successfully engaged in farming and associated craft activities.

In the 15th century, the town grew rapidly due to the port (then known as Porto Clementino), and trade with Provence and Sicily. Along with neighbouring Tuscany, these two regions exercised a great influence over the local artistic output. The particularly favourable economic climate attracted new Jewish families. According to local tradition, they mainly lived in the area near the Palazzo Comunale.

A tax register of 1470 recorded nine families of Jewish contributors. Thus, along with Viterbo, it was the largest Jewish community in the region. In the late 15th century, the town underwent an economic crisis due to the port gradually being landlocked, and it once more became a rural town. The Jewish group was reduced in numbers and by 1484 there were only five families left.

Interesting evidence to the Jewish presence may be found on the outer walls of the left aisle in the church of Santa Maria in Castello (begun in 1143 and completed in 1208): a decoration with candelabra akin to the Jewish *menorah*.

Terracina

Inhabitants 30,000
Altitude 22 m
Province of Latina
Itinerary 2

Situated at the foot of the Ausoni mountains rising up from the Pontine plain not far from the Via Appia, the initial Tuscan settlement was called *Tarracina* (the etymology is obscure). A fishing port and rural market town, today Terracina is also a busy seaside resort.

The Via Appia cuts right through the middle of the town, temporarily changing name to Via Roma and Via Marconi, and is interrupted by Piazza Garibaldi and Piazza della Repubblica. The town has two main parts: the upper mediaeval area and the modern port settlement.

In the lower part of the town, along the canal Pio vi leading to the sea, the remains of a Roman amphitheatre, baths and villas are surrounded by modern buildings, which have sprung up along the flat area as far as the promenade. By taking Via Roma you come to Piazza Garibaldi, designed by Luigi Valadier (1791-1831), with the war memorial at its centre and on one side the Neoclassical church of *Santissimo Salvatore*. Continuing to the main square, Piazza della Repubblica, you come first to Via Cavour and then Porta Napoli (or 14 Settembre), the southern entrance to the town on the Via Appia. The gate is dominated by the steep cliff called Pisco Montano.

By taking the Salita della Annunziata from Piazza Garibaldi you can go up to the medieval quarter. On the way up you come to the remains of the 14th-century church of the *Annunziata*, architectural fragments and inscriptions from Roman times and, before entering Piazza del Municipio, the remains of a four-sided stone arch. The heart of the historic centre, Piazza del Municipio, is built over the ancient forum, called the *Foro Emiliano*. This was a Jewish quarter in the 16th century until the expulsion.

The square has a number of fine buildings: the majestic cathedral of *San Cesario*, the Gothic *Palazzo Venditti* and the *Palazzo del Municipio* with the *Torre Frumentaria* or dei Rosa, now an archaeological museum.

By going down the adjacent Corso Anita Garibaldi, you come to the remains of the *Capitolium*, a 1st-century Roman temple, and the church of the *Purgatorio*, whose facade is adorned by gargoyles. A series of medieval houses lines the street as far as Porta Maggiore, the entrance to the ancient town. Beyond this gate, along large stretches of town walls is the Via Anxur rising up as far as the temple of Jupiter Anxur. At the top of the hill there is a fine view stretching from the promontory of Circeo below to the islands in the Ponza archipelago.

In a letter (Epistle xxxiv) to Pietro, Bishop of Terracina, Pope Gregory the Great ordered the re-opening of the synagogue, closed on the grounds that the prayers disturbed the services in the nearby church. The pope condemned this intolerant behaviour, claiming it 'terrorised' the Jews rather than bringing them nearer to the Christian faith. He thus charged the Bishop of Fondi to investigate personally and, if necessary, find a new place of worship for the Jews.

Historic sources suggest that the synagogue was in the ancient forum beside the cathedral. The outcome of the controversy is not known. The episode is important, however, since it confirms that there was a large Jewish colony in Terracina as early as the 6th century. They were attracted to the town by the potential for trade in the port.

Moneylenders benefited from favourable conditions approved by various popes. Pope Pius II invited the inhabitants of Terracina to welcome the Jews so that the city could obtain loans easily after the wars between Alfonso and Ferdinand I of Aragon.

On arriving from Majorca, Moshe Remos was employed as the teacher in the local community at a salary of 6 florins per year.

Many manuscripts were either written or purchased for leading figures in the local community, including *Saraval*, a manuscript by Mordekhai, son of Shmuel, and a manuscript written in Florence by Shimshon Zarfathi for Menachem, son of Meshullam from Terracina.

In the 16th century Terracina had one of the largest Jewish communities in the Marittima province, since ten households were taxed. After the bull of Paul IV, enclosing Jews in the ghettos, the Jewish houses were not separated from the Christian dwellings because, due to the opposition of the citizens, the town council was unable to grant the necessary accommodation.

After the definitive expulsion, there was no more mention of Jews until the 18th century, when for markets or fairs Jews were occasionally allowed to stay in Terracina for a maximum of three days.

Terracina is a common Roman Jewish surname (→ Segni/Jewish surnames).

Tivoli

Inhabitants 46,500
Altitude 235 m
Province of Rome
Itinerary 1

Situated on the river Aniene at the foot of the Tiburtini mountains, the ancient settlement of *Tibur* was – according to legend – founded by the Arcadian Catillus. An industrial centre, the town is often visited by day-trippers because of its proximity to Rome.

The historic centre of the town includes a number of interesting churches, such as *Santa Maria Maggiore* (built in the 5th century and re-structured several times in later periods), *San Silvestro* (12th century, with 14th-century frescoes inside), the 14th-century *Duomo* (with fine wooden statues) and *San Giovanni Evangelista* (with 16th-century frescoes). There are also a number of ancient Roman ruins, such as the *Temple of Vesta* (1st century BCE), which has a circular plan and columns with Corinthian capitals and friezes.

But the main attraction at Tivoli are its villas with gardens, fountains, and cascades. The grounds of *Villa d'Este* has 500 fountains making spectacular use of water from the Aniene, while the river itself plunges through the park of the *Villa Gregoriana* in powerful cascades.

The first mention of a Jewish group in Tivoli comes from the town statutes of 1305, a town decree of 1308 and several other official town documents. As in other Lazio towns, the Jews mainly engaged in moneylending and pawnbroking. The documents speak

Tivoli, detail of a fresco in the church of San Silvestro depicting a group of Jews taking part in the notorious dispute with Bishop Sylvester

of Elia Vitale, who lent money to the town, and of Dactuli di Consiglio, who received a tunic as a pawn in 1387.

But the Tivoli Jews' main claim to fame was medicine. This won them so much respect that they enjoyed privileges, such as exemption from wearing the badge, which had become compulsory in 1389. Among the physicians was Elia di Sabato, who was granted a diploma of Roman citizenship from the pope, and the physicist Salomone, mentioned in a sepulchral inscription brought to light in 1737 on the Via Tiburtina. Written in Hebrew, the epigraph commemorates his wife Rachele. Another illustrious physician was Mose da Tivoli, who successfully applied to Pope Innocent VII to have his *littera civilitatis* validated.

In the 15th century the community evidently had a high cultural level. This is demonstrated by the many manuscripts now in major libraries written by Mordekhai, son of Izhak di Tivoli, and by Shabbethai, son of Jehoshua di Tivoli. Moreover, Tivoli was the town chosen for a meeting of representatives from the Italian Jewish communities convened to discuss the anti-Jewish laws emanated by the Council of Basel (1431-49).

The Jewish community had its first cemetery in a place called Magnano three kilometres from the town centre, downhill from the present-day Via Tiburtina. In a later period archive sources mention a cemetery in the vicinity of 'the towers of Rocca Pia, near Parchetto (Barchetto) and precisely where there is still a large railing round the vegetable garden belonging to the warden of the current prison'. The synagogue, on the other hand, must have been in 'Palatiis', in the area between present-day Via Palatina and Vicolo dei Granai. For a while the latter street was also known as Via dei Giudii. Incorporated into other buildings, after various transformations, the synagogue building was eventually demolished in 1937 during works

to widen the Via Palatina. Presumably the Jewish quarter was near the synagogue in the Castrovetere area.

In the church of San Silvestro there is a 13th-century fresco depicting a group of Jews, albeit dressed in medieval clothes, taking part in the famous dispute with Bishop Sylvester of 315. A similar episode is represented in the church of Santi Quattro Corona, Rome (→ Rome/ Itinerary IV).

Not far from Tivoli, **Subiaco** almost certainly had at least an isolated Jewish presence, perhaps a single household, which for almost a century lived in the town and paid tax.

Tuscania

Inhabitants 7,500
Altitude 165
Province of Viterbo
Itinerary 3

Situated at the edge of the Volsini mountains, the ancient settlement was called *Tuscan* (from the word *etrusco* meaning 'Etruscan'). In the 15th century the town was disparagingly referred to as *Toscanella* ('Little Tuscan') by Pope Boniface VIII and this name stuck until 1911, when it reverted to its old name. Today the rural town also has some manufacturing industries, built outside the historic centre enclosed by the ancient walls.

Our visit to the historic centre begins from Porta San Marco and a long street running right through the town with various names: Via Marconi, Via Cavour, Via Rivellino and beyond Piazza Basile, Via del Comune. By turning out of Via Marconi into Via Settembre XX you come to the Largo Bixio and the 18th-century church of *San Marco*, remodelled in the mid 19th century. From the adjacent Largo della Rosa, the street goes down to the Romanesque church of *Santa Maria della Rosa* with its squat lateral bell tower.

By taking various streets from Via Marconi you come to Piazza Conte Enrico Pocci and the 15th-century church of *Sant'Agostino* (renovated in the 19th-century) with, inside, a fine cycle of frescoes. By taking Via Consalve you come to the ancient cathedral. Remodelled in the 19th century, it houses 16th-century statues and paintings. Some of the surrounding streets, especially Via Roma and Via Torre di Lavello are lined by former noble palaces. Having taken Via Garibaldi and the nearby Via Oberdan you come to Piazza Basile with the former church of *Santa Croce* (now the historical town archives and the library), the *Palazzo Comunale*, and the 15th-century church of *Santi Martiri* (or *San Lorenzo*) restored in the 19th century. A little off the beaten track but still inside the town walls, is the chapel of *San Francesco*.

A visit to Tuscania is not complete without seeing the three large churches outside the town walls. The first is the Renaissance church of *Santa Maria del Riposo* with annexed Franciscan monastery and Renaissance cloister, now the *Museo Nazionale di Arte Etrusca e Medievale*, reached from the Porta San Marco by going all the way along Viale Trieste. The other two churches are the former cathedral, the Romanesque *Santa Maria Maggiore* with its finely preserved harmoniously frescoed interior, and the Romanesque-Lombard church of *San Pietro*, once the town museum. Both these churches are reached by going from Via del Comune to the Porta del Poggio and then taking the provincial road for Viterbo.

The first Roman Jews probably settled in Toscanella (now Tuscan) at the beginning of the 14th century. At that time the town was growing thanks to the efficient administration under Cardinal Albornoz. The development continued in the second half of the century throughout the area.

Four families of Toscanella Jews were recorded in 1472 among the fifty Jewish contributors in the Patrimony of St Peter in Tuscia. They included some wealthy families, such as Manovello da Toscanella, who paid 41 ducats, and his brother Leuccio who paid 42.

The town moneylenders, like many of their colleagues in Tuscia, expanded their activities throughout the region. In 1489 a Jew from

Toscanella opened a loan-bank in Viterbo, managed by a certain Simuel.

The Jews of Toscanella not only ran their businesses. They also engaged in traditional Hebrew studies. Chronicles record the part played by a certain Rabbi Shemuel da Toscanella in an erudite dispute between rabbis at the turn of the 16th century. The controversy involved the followers of Menachem Recanati, the author of a commentary to the Torah (also studied by Pico della Mirandola), and some Spanish refugees on their way to Palestine. Among Recanati's opponents was the Toscanella rabbi, but we have no precise information about him. There are no visible traces of the Jewish past in the modern town of Tuscania.

Velletri

Inhabitants 25,000
Altitude 332 m
Province of Rome
Itinerary 1

Built on a spur of the Monte Artemisio, the ancient settlement was called *Velitrae* a name derived from an Etruscan root meaning 'upland'. A wine-producing centre, the historic town is well preserved and enjoys a wonderful view.

Our visit begins in Via Vittorio Emanuele, which cuts right through the town, and Piazza Cairoli with the Gothic-Romanesque *Torre di Trivio* and the 17th-century church of *Santa Maria del Trivio*. The nearby Via del Comune leads to Piazza del Comune dominated by the 16th-century *Palazzo Comunale*, now the town museum; the palace facade is by Vignola (1507-73).

Behind the town hall, after Via Borgia and Piazza Mazzini, you come to Piazza Umberto with its arcades and the 13th-century cathedral of *San Clemente*. Alongside, under the arcade, is the *Museo Capitolare*, housing collections of paintings, miniatures, gold works and sacred vestments.

In 1391 the people of Rome granted the citizens of Velletri, including the Jews, a safe conduct for the city of Rome and its territory valid for two years. This document specified that the inhabitants of Velletri could take part in the Testaccio games and that the Jews had to contribute sums of money to them.

Given the amount of taxes paid to the papal collectors, the Velletri community must have been one of the largest in Lazio. A 15th-century notarial deed indicates the synagogue as being in the Portella area. The Jews also probably lived in this area, bounded by what is now Via della Stamperia, Via della Trinità and Vicolo del Serpe, formerly Via della Sinagoga.

In 1547 with the consent of the town authorities, a Jewish loan-bank was opened. According to the statutes, the Jews could live outside the Jewish quarter and set up a synagogue inside one of their own houses. Two years later the concession was revoked and the town council decreed the expulsion of Jews from Velletri, but this ruling was probably not applied immediately, since moneylending continued in the town for some time afterwards.

We can be certain that not all the Jews left, because in 1569 the Community provided the flag for the town militia at its own expense. From 1558 to 1570, thirty-six children were circumcised by the physician Jechiel Manoscrivi, who drafted his *Chochmat Nashim* in Velletri. Because of the more liberal regime compared to Rome, many Jews from surrounding towns sought refuge in Velletri.

In 1587 four new loan-banks were opened and remained in business until the definitive expulsion, decreed by Pope Clement VII. With more or less temporary permits Jews were allowed to return to Velletri in the 19th century to sell their wares at the fair of San Clemente.

According to a letter of 1862, the Modigliani family had enjoyed the exceptional privilege of living permanently in the town for over a century.

In nearby **Lanuvio**, the only surviving evidence of a Jewish presence may be found in the archives. Given the amount of taxes paid by Jews, however, the community must have been fairly large. It had a synagogue, and social and economic life was governed by the town statutes. The archives reveal that in 1475 a Jewish barley merchant was working in the town.

Velletri, a building in the Decarcia Portella, *now Via della Stamperia*

Velletri, detail of the rose window in the building in Via della Stamperia

Veroli

Veroli, Vicolo San Nicola

*Veroli, Via Franco dei Franconi,
detail of the symbolic pomegranate
on the building identified as
the old synagogue*

Inhabitants 3,500
Altitude 594
Province of Frosinone
Itinerary 2

Situated at the foot of the Ernici mountains, the original Etruscan settlement was called *Verulae*. Today it is an important market town for a widespread rural community. The town has a number of ancient monuments and a medieval quarter.

Our visit begins in Piazzale Vittorio Veneto with the war memorial and continues to Largo Arneari. We then go from Via Gracilia to Via Sulpicio, crossing a number of streets lined by imposing medieval and Renaissance palaces as far as the Porta Romana, where you can enjoy a fine panoramic view. By taking Via Garibaldi you reach the Romanesque church of *Sant'Erasmo*, built over a former Benedictine monastery and remodelled in the 18th century. Back in Largo Arenara, you turn into Corso M. Fortunata Viti, where you can admire the paintings in the church of the *Annunziata* (or *Sant'Agostino*), and the medieval *Casa Reali*. In this 'royal house' there is a rare example of a Roman calendar from the Augustan age incorporated in the loggia walls. Having reached Piazza Duomo you enter Piazza Mazzini. Here are the *Palazzo Comunale*, and, standing alone, the Romanesque cathedral of *Sant'Andrea Apostolo*. Behind, in a small square, is another church, the 13th-century *Santa Maria Salome*, and, opposite, the *Palazzo del Seminario*, which houses a library, the *Biblioteca Civica Giovardina* founded in 1773 by Monsignor Vittorio Giovardi. After coming back to the cathedral, you can take Via dei Franconi to a small square with the Romanesque church of *Santa Maria dei Franconi* and the 18th-century elliptical church of the *Benedettine*.

A copy of the Veroli town statutes (1657) mentions Jews in some of the measures, significantly emphasising prohibitions and restrictions. In particularly adamant terms the Christians were prohibited from buying grapes or must (fermenting grape juice) from Jews. The concern that the Jewish malediction – *hebraica malitia* – could contaminate the consecration of wine used in celebrating Mass is expressed in great detail.

The Jewish community was not particularly large, although in 1472 it did consist of four households making a total of around 24-30 people. In the cadastre of 1546, most of the Jews were defined as *inabile* (unfit). Despite this precarious situation the Veroli Jews established at least two schools in 1538 and 1547.

The synagogue was in a 15th-century house near the main square: the building currently at no. 3 Via Franco dei Franconi. This building has a number of unusual decorative motifs, including the symbol for the pomegranate and a low relief, almost completely effaced but identified as a *mezuzah* on the jamb of the next-door building (no. 5). The house belonged to the Caetani family, the *signori* of Campagna, who showed a tolerant attitude towards Jews.

In 1486 the workshop of Sabatuccio di Maestro Leuccio (one of the most influential men in the small Veroli community) was situated in Contrada di San Nicola, near the public road, and his rented house – the lease was signed in 1505 – was in the Castello area.

Veroli is one of the most common Jewish surnames (→ Segni/Jewish surnames).

The town statutes of nearby **Ferentino** included as many as eleven clauses referring to Jews. This is evidence that there had been a long-standing significant Jewish presence.

As in Veroli, here, too, the statutes mention the usual rules, but are particularly severe. Thus while Christian wet nurses caught feeding a Jewish baby were usually fined, at Ferentino they were whipped.

Despite the difficult situation, five Jewish households figured in the tax survey of 1472. In addition to official moneylending, these families engaged in trade of various goods, including foodstuffs, thus blatantly contravening the usual prohibitions.

From 1472 to 1485, the Jew Mele provided the whole town with material which today we would call stationery – paper, account books, and wax for seals – as well as other material such as steel for repairing the public mills, oil for the lighting in the town hall, bread and wine. The Jewish community was also involved in tax collecting.

Mele, the 'town supplier', and his family lived beside the Piazza del Comune near the slaughterhouse in the parish of San Valentino; his name appears on the sales deed for the house.

Generally speaking the Jewish community was fairly well-off. It also reached a high cultural level, as is demonstrated by two sheets in a small paper manuscript of 1510, found in a notarial protocol in the town archives: a perpetual lunar calendar written in Italian-style Hebrew handwriting.

Viterbo, Via San Lorenzo,
the street which had Jewish shops
in the late 15th century

Viterbo

Inhabitants 59,000
Altitude 326 m
Itinerary 3

Situated along the Via Cassia on a hill between the Cimini and Volsini mountains, this provincial capital has preserved its ancient Roman name meaning 'old city'. Today a commercial and industrial centre, Viterbo is also a communications junction between Rome and Tuscany and between the Tyrrhenian coast and the Tiber valley. The historic centre is still enclosed by the ancient walls.

Our visit begins from the stage-like Piazza del Plebiscito, the political and administrative heart of the medieval town, with the 16th-century *Palazzo Comunale* (interior with frescoes), the 14th-century *Palazzo del Podestà*, surmounted by a slender tower, *the Palazzo della Prefettura* and the Romanesque church of *Sant'Angelo in Spata*. In the 16th century the large Viterbo Jewish community lived in this area.

By going along Via San Lorenzo you reach the adjacent Via Chigi and the 17th-century Palazzo Chigi with its porticoed court. Back in Via San Lorenzo, you come to the medieval *Torre di Borgognone*. In Piazza del Gesù, lined by medieval houses with external stairs, is the Romanesque church of the *Gesu*.

The next stop is the triangular Piazza della Morte with the Romanesque *Loggia di San Tommaso* and, alongside, the recent modern church of the Morte. Beyond the Ponte del Duomo with its rows of Etruscan stones, you come to the 15th-century *Palazzo Farnese*. This building is said to be the birthplace of Alessandro

Viterbo, Hebrew funerary inscription (1401) commemorating Reuben, a 'sensible and graceful' boy who died aged seven (Museo Civico)

Farnese, Pope Paul III (1834-49). Having gone past Etruscan wall remains, you enter Piazza San Lorenzo, the religious hub of the medieval town with the Romanesque cathedral of *San Lorenzo*, the medieval *Palazzo Papale* and the broad loggia with overlapping series of arches. Back in Piazza della Morte, you take Via San Pellegrino to explore the medieval quarter with its alleys, well-preserved towers, houses, and decorations. The street ends at the Porta San Pietro, one of the gateways in the imposing town walls round the historic centre. By continuing along a stretch of wall, you can get back to the centre through the Porta Romana, beside the Romanesque church of *San Sisto*. By taking Via Garibaldi, you come to the Piazza della Fontana Grande, with its 13th-century fountain. From here you go behind Via Cavour, also called Via Nova, lined by medieval houses, to reach Via Saffi and the 15th-century *Casa Poscia* characterised by dark stone and external stairs.

Having come back to Piazza del Plebiscito, you can begin the visit to the northern quarter of the town, built more recently, but still inside the town walls. The first square you come to is Piazza delle Erbe with its 17th century *Fontana dei Leoni*. You then go past the Renaissance houses in Via dell'Orologio Vecchio. From here, after Via Mazzini, you come to Piazza Alighieri (with a 13th-century fountain) and an impressive palace, now a bank, *Palazzo della Cassa di Risparmio* (inside are frescoes and a picture gallery), and the Romanesque church of *San Giovanni in Zoccoli*.

Having reached the Porta della Verità, you go beyond the walls to visit the 14th-century church of *Santa Maria della Verità* and the former convent, now a museum, the *Museo Civico*. After going along a stretch of the town walls, you go back into the historic centre along Via Rosselli as far as Piazza Verdi, one of the principal squares in the town. On the sides of the square are the Neoclassical *Teatro dell'Unione*, the 16th-century *Palazzo Santoro*, now housing the Biblioteca Comunale degli Ardenti and the medieval church of *San Marco*, with frescoes and paintings inside. Having taken Via Santa Rosa, you come to the sanctuary of Santa Rosa, destroyed in the 17th century and then rebuilt in Neoclassical style in the 19th century.

From Piazza Verdi, you go along Via Matteotti as far as the Piazza della Rocca (with a 16th-century fountain), dominated by the 15th-century *Rocca* (fort), which was restored after being seriously damaged in the Second World War. Opposite the Rocca is another gateway – the Porta Fiorentina.

By taking Via San Francesco, you reach the Gothic church of the *San Francesco*. By going in the opposite direction, along Via Cairoli, you reach the Piazza San Faustino e Giovita with a 14th-century fountain and the 18th-century church dedicated to the saints of the same name (paintings and frescoes inside). Lastly, after enjoying the fine views along Via Santa Maria Liberatrice, you come to the large 14th-century sanctuary-church of the *Santissima Trinità* and its Renaissance cloister. From here you take a number of side streets back to the main square, Piazza del Plebiscito.

At the bottom of a 13th-century Hebrew manuscript in the Biblioteca Casantense, Rome (ms. 3088), is the name of a proprietor in both Latin and Hebrew: Joseph, son of Mordekhai from Viterbo. A notarial deed from the same period mentions Iudas Danielis, a Jew from Viterbo. In the early 15th century some Jews had already been involved in such serious incidents that the town had been excommunicated and had received the papal interdiction, only eventually revoked thanks to the mediation of the Bishop of Teramo. Although obliged to wear the badge (a red cloth circle for men, and a yellow veil for women), the Viterbo Jews could live anywhere in the town, but actually chose to reside in a group in the streets around the Palazzo Comunale, perhaps because living together afforded greater protection. Some 15th-century documents record that Viterbo Jews lived in the Contrada San Biagio near the modern Via Lafontaine. A document of 1491 mentions the synagogue in the Contrada San Silvestro and in 1494 another synagogue is mentioned as being in the Contrada San Simeone, the area of the present-day Via dell'Orologio. There are known to have been Jewish shops in Via San Lorenzo.

The Viterbo Jews must have been fairly wealthy, judging by the register of taxes paid to the Apostolic Chamber. The Viterbo contributors paid the most taxes of all Jews in the region. In 1440 however, the town authorities decided to reduce drastically Jewish taxes, to ease their difficulties due to an economic and demographic crisis. There were very close contacts between Viterbo and Romans Jews through business and family relations. One of the most important families in the community was that of Leuccio da Ventura. He was protected by the Gatti family, the victors in the struggle for power in the town.

Following the bull of Paul IV in 1555, the Jews were confined in a special quarter, later closed by a gate. The quarter was in Valle Piatta, inside the walls at Porta Faul. This was the site of the so-called 'Jewish baths', one of the ancient fountains previously used by the Romans as public baths. Beyond the gate there was a hillock known as the 'Jewish mound', probably used as a burial place. In all likelihood, the Hebrew funeral epitaph of 1401, now in the Museo Civico, came from this place. The epigraph concerns Reuben, son of Nethanel Chaim, a child who had died at the age of seven.

The Viterbo Jews had a very lively intellectual life. Significantly, Cardinal Egidio was from Viterbo. In the 16th century he was the most important exponent of the so-called 'Christian Cabbala', a Christian version of Hebrew mysticism.

In the Viterbo town library there are a number of important printed Hebrew works. Frequent allusions to

Viterbo, Via Cardinal Lafayette

mysticism and the Hebrew tradition are to be found in the writings of Annio da Viterbo, a minor intellectual who lived from the end of the 15th century to the early 16th century. In one of Annio's writings there is a Jewish character, possibly fictitious, called Rabbi Samuel who, together with the author, was the leading player in a very spurious episode: the 'Chaldean epigraph' supposedly discovered by Annio and translated by Samuel. For a certain period Flavio Mitridate, a converted Sicilian Jew and leading figure in Renaissance culture, lived in Viterbo.

In the following centuries until 1569, the year of the definitive expulsion, whenever the papal measures slackened, Jews returned to the places where they had lived, to trade as travelling salesmen in the local fairs. In 1705 Some Jews from Rome and areas around Viterbo, who had come for a fair, were accused of a ritual murder. Appointed by the Rome Community, Rabbi Tranquillo Vita Corcos took their defence and obtained an acquittal. After the unity of Italy, the Jews went to Viterbo mainly for happier reasons. The town and especially the hostelry called *Locanda dell'Angeletto* were mentioned as frequent destinations for honeymoon couples in a sonnet by Crescenzo Del Monte, the most famous 19th-century Jewish Roman dialect poet.

Vitorchiano, no. 28 Via Ugolini is known as the 'rabbi's house'

There are a number of archive documents attesting to a Jewish presence in the nearby towns of **Vetralla** and **Bagnaia**. According to these parchments from 15th-century liturgical codices, there was a synagogue in Bagnaia, which paid ten scudi to the House of the Catechumens in 1569. **Vitorchiano** also has some sporadic documents mentioning the Jewish presence in the town. In the inventory of the old town archives and notarial deeds there is a receipt for a payment made by Jews, and a deed for a payment made to the House of Catechumens. Today a house in the town – no. 28 Via Ugolini – is still known as the 'Rabbi's House'.

Selected Bibliography

For books of general interest, we suggest:

Encylopaedia Judaica, 16 vols., Jerusalem, Keter, 1971 (with subsequent supplements).
MILANO A., *Storia degli ebrei in Italia,* Turin, Einaudi, 1963.
Rassegna Mensile d'Israel, Rome, 1925... (henceforth cited as RMI).
Guida d'Italia, Lazio, Milan, TCI, 1996.

For in-depth studies on Jews in Lazio, we recommend the following texts:

CACIORGNA M. T., 'Presenza ebraica nel Lazio meridionale: il caso di Sermoneta', in *Aspetti e problemi della presenza ebraica nell'Italia centro-meridionale (secoli XIV-XV)*, Quaderni dell'Istituto di Scienze storiche dell'Università di Roma, no. 2, Rome 1983.

DI CASTRO D. (ed.), *Arte ebraica a Roma e nel Lazio*, Palombi, Rome, 1994.

ESPOSITO A., 'Consuetudini, vita e normative per gli ebrei della Regione di Campagna alla fine del Medioevo', in *Statuti e ricerca storica*, conference proceedings, Ferentino 11-13 March 1988, Comune di Ferentino Assessorato alla cultura, Quaderni di storia, no. 8, Ferentino 1990.

ESPOSITO A., 'Una descriptio relativa all presenza ebraica nel Lazio meridionale', in *Latium* 2, 1985.

ESPOSITO A., 'Prestito ebraico e Monti di Pietà dei territori pontifici nel tardo Quattrocento: il caso di Rieti', in *Credito e sviluppo economico in Italia dal Medioevo all'età contemporanea*, Società italiana degli storici dell'economia, Verona 1988.

ESPOSITO A., 'La presenza ebraica in una regione pontificia nel tardo Medioevo: Viterbo e il Patrimonio di S. Pietro in Tuscia', in *Italia Judaica*, proceedings for the VI international conference, Ministero per i beni culturali e ambientali, Ufficio centrale beni archivistici, Tel Aviv, 18-23 January 1995, forthcoming.

ESPOSITO A., 'La presenza ebraica in Sabina nel tardo Medioevo', proceedings of the Magliano Sabina conference (June 1995), forthcoming.

ESPOSITO A., PROCACCIA M., 'La schola siciliana de Urbe, la fine della storia?', in *Italia Judaica*, 'Gli ebrei in Sicilia sino all'espulsione del 1492', proceedings of the V international conference, Palermo, 15-19 June 1992, Ministero per i beni culturali e ambientali, Ufficio centrale beni archivistici, Rome 1995.

'Gli ebrei a Cori nella prima metà del '500', in *Ypothekai*, III, 102, January-April / April-August 1987.

LEVI CAVAGLIONE P., *Guerriglia nei Castelli Romani*, Einaudi, Turin 1945.

LUZZATTI M., *La casa dell'ebreo*, Nistri-Lischi, Pisa 1985.

PAVONCELLO N., 'Le comunità ebraiche laziali prima del bando di Pio V', in *Lunario romano* IX, 1980.

PESIRI G., 'La schola e le case de li Iudej di Fondi', in *Confronti* 11, 1996.

PROCACCIA M., '"Talmudistae caballarii" e Annio', in *Cultura umanistica a Viterbo*, Università degli studi della Tuscia, Viterbo 1991.

PROCACCIA M., 'Gli ebrei a Sermoneta fino alla metà del Cinquecento', proceedings of the conference 'Sermoneta e i Caetani', Rome, June 1994, forthcoming.

STRIPE M., 'Una sinagoga a Veroli', in *Lazio ieri e oggi*, XX, 3, 1984.

TOAFF A., 'Gli ebrei romani e il commercio del denaro nei comuni dell'Italia meridionale alla fine del

Duecento', in *Italia Judaica*, proceedings of the I international conference, Bari, 18-22 May 1981, Ministero per i beni culturali e ambientali, Ufficio centrale beni archivistici, Rome 1983.

For in-depth studies on Jews in Rome, we recommend the following texts:

ASCARELLI A., *Le Fosse Ardeatine*, Rome, ANFIM, 1989.

BINYAMIN DA TUDELA, *Itinerario*, Italian trans. by G. Busi, Rimini, Luisé, 1987.

BENOCCI C., GUIDONI E. (ed.), *Il ghetto. Atlante storico della città italiane, Roma, 2*, Rome, Bonsignori, 1993.

BERLINER A., *Storia degli ebrei di Roma*, Milan, Rusconi, 1992 (Frankfurt 1893).

BLUSTEIN G., *Storia degli ebrei in Roma*, Rome, Maglione e Strini, 1921.

BUSI G., *Libri e scrittori nella Roma ebraica del Medioevo*, Rimini, Luisé, 1990.

COSTA V., ARMANNI O., *Il nuovo Tempio israelitico di Roma*. Relazione al Consiglio di Presidenza e alla Commissione Tecnico-Amministrativa dell'Università Israelitica Romana, Rome, Tip. Giovanni Balbi, 1904.

CAVIGLIA S., *L'identità salvata. Gli ebrei di Roma tra fede e nazione, 1870-1938*, Rome-Bari, Laterza, 1996.

COEN F., *16 ottobre 1943. La grande razzia degli ebrei a Roma*, Florence, La Giuntina, 1993.

D'AZEGLIO M., *Sull'emancipazione civile degli israeliti*, Florence, Memonnier, 1848.

DE BENEDETTI G., *16 ottobre 1943*, Rome, Editori Riuniti, 1985.

DI CASTRO D. (ed.), *Arte ebraica a Roma e nel Lazio*, Rome, Palombi, 1994.

DE SEGNI R., 'Nuovi dati sugli incunaboli ebraici di Roma', *Un pontificato e una città, Sisto IV (1471-1484)*, conference proceedings, Rome 3-7 December 1984, Rome, 1986.

DE SEGNI R., *Il Vangelo del ghetto*, Rome, Newton Compton, 1985.

1870. La breccia del ghetto. Evoluzione degli ebrei di Roma, Rome, Barulli, 1971.

ESPOSITO A., *Un'altra Roma, Minoranze nazionali e comunità ebraiche tra Medioevo e Rinascimento*, Rome, Il Calamo, 1995.

FOA A., SILVERA M., STOW K. (ed.), 'Oltre il 1492', in *RMI*, LVIII, 1-2, 1992.

FORNARI S., *La Roma del ghetto*, Rome, Palombi, 1984.

FREUD S., *Moses and Monotheism*, New York, Random House, 1987.

GELLER H., GELLER R., *Roma ebraica. Duemila anni di storia in immagini*, Rome, Viella, 1984.

GREGOROVIUS F., *Passeggiate per l'Italia*, Rome, Carboni, 1907.

Il ghetto di Roma. Progetto di recupero urbano ed edilizio. Regione Lazio, Assessorato ai Lavori Pubblici, Rome, Edizioni Kappa, 1995.

MANN V. B. (ed.), *I Tal yà. Isola della rugiada divina, Duemila anni di arte e vita ebraica in Italia*, Milan, Mondadori, 1990.

MIGLIAU B., 'Nuove prospettive di studio sulle Cinque Scole del ghetto di Roma: l'identificazione e il recupero dell'aron di Scola Catalana', in *Henoch*, XXI, 2, 1990.

MIGLIAU B., PROCACCIA M., 'La documentazione della scuola media ebraica di Roma del 1938', in *Italia Judaica, Gli ebrei nell'Italia unita (1870-1943)*, proceedings of the IV international conference, Siena 12-16 June 1989, Rome 1993.

MILANO A., *Il ghetto di Roma*, Rome, Staderini, 1964; Rome, Carucci, 1988.

MILANO A., 'Il cimitero ebraico sull'Aventino', in *RMI*, IX, 5-6, 1934.

NEHER-BERNHEIM R., *L'ebraismo nel mondo romano*, Milan, Editrice Scuola della Comunità Israelitica di Milano, 1969.

PALADINI A., *Via Tasso carcere nazista*, Rome, Istituto Poligrafico e Zecca dello Stato, 1986.

PAVONCELLO N., 'L'antica sinagoga in Trastevere', in *RMI*, XXX, 11, 1964.

PAVONCELLO N., 'La sinagoga o Scola

dei Quattro capi a Roma', in *Studi Romani*, 33, 1-2, 1985.

PAVONCELLO N., 'L'antico cimitero ebraico di Trastevere', in *RMI*, XXXII, 5, 1966.

PETRUCCIOLI A. (ed.), *Sefarad. Architettura e urbanistica ebraiche dopo il 1492*, Como, Dell'Oca, 1993.

PICCIOTTO FARGION L., *L'occupazione tedesca e gli ebrei di Roma*, Rome, Carucci, 1979.

RACHELI A. M., 'Il "risanamento" del Ghetto. La demolizione e ricostruzione del quartiere del Ghetto (1885-1911)', in *Roma Capitale 1870-1911. Architettura e Urbanistica*, Venice, Marsilio, 1984.

Ricordo della consacrazione e inaugurazione del nuovo Tempio Israelitico di Roma, Rome, Casa editrice italiana, 1904.

SCHWARZFUCHS S., 'Controversie nella Comunità di Roma agli inizi del secolo XVI', in *Scritti in Memoria di Enzo Sereni*, Milan-Jerusalem, Sally Mayer Foundation, 1970.

SERVI S. (ed.), *Il Museo ebraico di Roma*, Rome, Comunità Israelitica di Roma, 1985.

STOW K., *The Jews in Rome, I, 1536-1551*, Leiden-New York-Koln, Brill, 1995.

TAGLIACOZZO F., MIGLIAU B., *Gli ebrei nella storia e nella società contemporanea*, Florence, La Nuova Italia, 1993.

The Jewish Presence in Ancient Rome, Jerusalem, Bible and Land Museum, 1994.

TOAFF A., 'Stampe rare della Biblioteca della Comunità Israelitica di Roma scampate al saccheggio nazisata', in *La bibliofilia*, LXXX, 2, 1978.

TOAFF A., 'Lotte e fazioni fra gli ebrei di Roma nel Cinquecento', in *Studi Romani*, 27, 1970.

TOAFF A., *Il ghetto di Roma nel Cinquecento. Conflitti etnici e problemi socio-economici*, Jerusalem, Bar-Ilan University Press, 1984 (in Hebrew with Italian summary).

TOAFF A., 'Gli ebrei siciliani in Italia dopo l'espulsione. Storia di una integrazione mancata', in *Italia Judaica, Gli ebrei in Sicilia sino all'espulsione del 1492*, proceedings of the V international conference, Palermo 15-19 June 1992, Rome 1995.

VIVANTI C. (ed.), *Storia d'Italia, Annali 11. Gli ebrei in Italia, I, Dal Medioevo all'età dei ghetti*, Turin, Einaudi, 1996.

SELECTED BIBLIOGRAPHY

Glossary

Adar
6th month in the Jewish calendar, falling around February and March.

Aliyah
[Ascension] 1. The stepping up to the podium in the synagogue to read the *Torah*. 2. The return of the Jews to Israel.

Amidah
Daily prayer of 18 benedictions recited while standing.

Ark, Holy Ark, Aron, or *Aron-Hakodesh*
A receptacle for the scrolls of the *Torah*.

Arvith
Evening prayer.

Ashkenazi (pl. *+zim*)
A Jew of German or East European descent.

Atarah (pl. *+roth*)
A crown adorning the *Torah*.

Av, or *Ab*
11th month in the Jewish calendar, falling around July and August.

Bar-Mitzvah, or *Bath-Mitzvah*
[Son or daughter of the law] 1. The ceremony marking the 13th birthday of a boy (or 12th birthday of a girl), who then assumes his (or her) full religious obligations; after the ceremony the boy may be included in the *Minyan*. 2. The boy (or girl) himself (or herself).

Baruch
Blessed; the first word in all blessings.

Berachah
Blessing, benediction.

Besamim
The scents used during the closing cermony on the Sabbath (*Havdalah*).

Beth Knesset
Synagogue.

Bimah, bima, or *bema*
A platform in a synagogue from which the Scriptures are read and prayers recited (see also *Tevah*).

Cabbala, or *kabbala*
[Tradition] An ancient Jewish mystical tradition based on an esoteric interpretation of the Old Testament.

Challah, or *hallah* (pl. *+lahs* or *+loth*)
White bread, usually in the form of a plaited loaf, eaten on the Sabbath.

Cohen (pl. *cohanim*)
Priest; descendant of Aaron.

Derashah
Sermon; interpretation.

Elul
12th month in the Jewish calendar, falling around August and September.

Eretz Israel
Land of Israel.

Feneration
[From Latin *fæneratio*] Lending money on interest; usury.

Gemara
The later (3rd-5th century CE) part of the *Talmud*, being a commentary on the *Mishnah*.

Goy (pl. *goyim*)
Gentile, non-Jew (slang).

Haftarah, or *haphtarah*
A reading from the Prophets recited or chanted during the services for Sabbaths and festivals.

Haggadah
[Story] The non-legal part of the *Talmud* literature (see *Halachah*). *Haggadah of Pesach*: the tale of the Exodus read during Passover.

Halachah, or *Halakah*
Jewish traditional law or body of traditional laws.

Hanukkah, or *Chanukah*
[Dedication] The eight-day festival of lights commemorating the rededication of the Temple by Judas Maccabaeus after the victory of the Maccabees over Antiochus IV of Syria in 164 BCE.

Hanukkiah
Lamp with eight candles, plus the *shammash*, symbolising the eight days of *Hanukkah*.

Haskalah
1. Knowledge, education. 2. The Jewish Enlightenment movement (*c.* 1750-1800).

Hasidism, or *Chasidism*
Popular Jewish mystic movement founded by Rabbi Israel Ba'al Shem Tov in Poland about 1750.

Hatzer, or *Chaser*
1. Courtyard; delimited neighbourhood. 2. Rabbinate seat.

Havdalah
[Separation] Closing ceremony on the Sabbath.

Hechal
1. Palace; the Temple. 2. Sanctuary; the Holy *Ark*.

Heshvan, or *Cheshvan*
2nd month in the Jewish calendar, falling around October and November.

Incunabulum (pl. *+la*)
Any book printed by movable type before 1500. The first such book was the Latin Bible printed by Gutenberg at Mainz in 1453-55 and now kept at the Mazarine Library, Paris.

Iyar, or *Iyyar*
8th month in the Jewish calendar, falling around April and May.

Kaddish (pl. *+shim*)
An ancient Jewish liturgical prayer, especially the one recited in memory of the dead.

Keter
Crown of the *Torah*.

Ketubah
Marriage contract.

Kiddush
[Sanctification] A ceremonial blessing recited over bread or a cup of wine on the Sabbath or a festival.

Kippah
Skullcap.

Kippur
Day of Atonement.

Kislev
3rd month in the Jewish calendar, falling around November and December.

Kosher, or *kasher*
[Proper] Prepared according to or conforming to Jewish dietary laws.

Levite
Descendant of the priestly tribe of Levi.

Lulav
1. Palm branch; one of the four plant species used on *Sukkoth*. 2. A bouquet made of three of these species – palm, myrtle and willow – to which the citron, or *ethrog*, must be added.

Machzor, or *mahzor* (pl. *+zorim*)
[Cycle] Prayer book containing prescribed holy day rituals.

Magen (or *Mogen*) *David*
Another name for the Star of David, a star with six points made of two joined triangles – the symbol of Judaism.

Mappah (pl. *+oth*)
Cloth used for wrapping the *Torah* during a pause in the reading.

Masorah, or *Massora*
[Tradition] The critical annotations for the biblical text; it is divided into magna, parva and finale.

Masoretic Decoration
Form of illumination in Spanish manuscripts of the 14th and 15th centuries, especially in the *Masorah*, where Hebrew letters were scribed to create graphic designs, such as likenesses, often grotesque, of animals, human faces, plants and fruits (in later German codices). This was a way of circumventing the Second Commandment, which forbids the creation of any likeness of God and inhibited the development of Jewish painting.

Matzah, or *matzo* (pl. +*zoth* or +*zos*)
A large brittle extra-thin biscuit of unleavened bread eaten during *Passover*.

Megillah (pl. +*lahs* or +*loth*)
Scroll. *Megillath Esther*: Scroll containing the Book of Esther. *The Five Megilloth*: The books of Esther, The Song of Solomon, Ruth, Lamentations and Ecclesiastes.

Meil (pl. +*lim*)
Ornamental cape used for the *Torah*.

Menorah
A seven-branched candelabrum used in ceremonies.

Mezuzah
A piece of parchment inscribed with scriptural passages and fixed to the doorpost of a Jewish house.

Midrash
[Search] The exposition and exegesis of a biblical text. *Bet ha-midrash*: Study house or rabbinical school.

Mikveh
Ritual bath.

Milah
Circumcision.

Minhah
Afternoon prayer.

Minyan (pl. +*nim*)
The number of persons required by Jewish law to be present at a religious service, i.e. at least ten males over the age of 13.

Mishnah
A collection of precepts passed down as an oral tradition and assembled by Judah ha-Nasi in the 2nd century CE. The earlier part of the *Talmud* (see also *Gemara*).

Mitzvah (pl. +*vahs* or +*voth*)
A commandment or precept.

Ner Tamid
Eternal candle, hung in front of the Holy *Ark*.

Nisan
The 7th month in the Jewish calendar, falling around March and April.

Omer
An ancient Hebrew measure, equal to about 4 litres; that measure of grain from the first harvest offered on the 2nd day of *Passover*. *Counting of the Omer*: The seven weeks from the second day of *Passover* to the first day of *Shabuoth*.

Parashah (pl. +*shoth*)
Any of the sections of the *Torah*, or of the weekly lessons, read on Sabbaths in the synagogue.

Parnas (pl. + im)
The administrator of a community.

Parocheth
Ornamental curtain hung in front of the Holy *Ark*.

Passover, or *Pesach*
Eight-day celebration of the Exodus from Egypt. During the festival the eating of leavened bread is forbidden and, instead, the *matzah* is eaten. Passover opens with the *Seder*.

Phylacteries, or *teffilin*
Two small leather cases containing strips of parchment inscribed with religious texts, worn by men during morning prayer.

Pluteus
A cabinet and bookrest where precious books of a library are kept.

Purim
[Lots] A carnival festival on *Adar* 14 celebrating the rescue of the Jews in Persia by Queen Esther, and during which the *Megillath Esther* is read.

Rimmonim
[Pomegranates] Silver ferrules, usually in the form of pomegranates, which were once used to decorate the *Torah*.

Rosh Hashanah
The Jewish New Year, marked by the blowing of the *shofar*. *Rosh Hashanah La'Ilanot*: The New Year for the Trees.

Seder
[Order] A ceremonial dinner with ritual reading of the Haggadah observed on the first night of *Passover*.

Sefer (pl. *Sefarim*)
Book. *Sefer Torah* (pl. *Sifre Torah*): The scroll of the Torah containing the Pentateuch.

Sephardi (pl. +*dim*)
A Jew of Spanish, Portuguese or North African descent.

Shaddai
[The Almighty, God] a medallion or talisman made of the Hebrew letters of the word and hung on a baby's crib or around the neck.

Shammash, or *shammes*
1. Rabbi's assistant during the holy services. 2. The extra (9th) candle used on the Feast of *Hanukkah* to light the other eight candles of the *Hanukkiah*.

Shabuoth, or *Shavuot*
[Weeks] The Feast of Weeks or Pentecost, celebrated on the 6th day of *Sivan* to commemorate the revelation of the *Torah* and the giving of the Ten Commandments to Moses on Mount Sinai.

Shemini Atzereth
The eighth and last day of *Sukkoth*.

Shevat, or *Shebat*
5th month in the Jewish calendar, falling around January and February.

Shofar
Ram's horn, blown during *Rosh Hashanah* and other ceremonies.

Siddur
A year-round prayer book, for weekdays, holidays and Sabbaths.

Simhath Torah
[Rejoicing of the Torah] A celebration marking the completion of the yearly cycle of *Torah* readings at the synagogue.

Sivan
9th month in the Jewish calendar, falling around May and June.

Sukkah
Tabernacle in which *Sukkoth* is celebrated.

Sukkoth, or *Succoth*
[Tabernacles] An eight-day harvest festival commemorating the period when the Israelites lived in the wilderness.

Tallith (pl. +*lithim*)
A white shawl with fringed corners worn over the head and shoulders by Jewish men at prayer.

Talmud
[Instruction] The main authoritative compilation of ancient Jewish law and tradition comprising the *Mishnah* and the *Gemara*. *Talmud Torah*: School where boys are taught the Torah.

Tammuz, or *Thammuz*
10th month in the Jewish calendar, falling around June and July.

Tanach
The Jewish Bible, divided into the Pentateuch (*Torah*), the Prophets (*Neviim*) and the Hagiographa (*Ketuvim*) [the word is an acronym of the Hebrew initials of its three parts].

Targum
An Aramaic translation of sections of the Old Testament.

Tashlikh
[You shall cast] In this ceremony on the first day of Rosh Hashanah sins committed are symbolically thrown into the sea or a river. The term comes from the prophet Micah (7.19).

Tass (pl. +*sim*)
Ornamental tray for the *Torah*.

Tefillah
Prayer; specifically the *Amidah*.

Tefillin
See *Phylacteries*.

Tevah
A platform in a synagogue from which the Scriptures are read and prayers recited (see also *Bimah*).

Tevet, or *Tebet*
4th month of the Jewish calendar, falling around December and January.

Tiq
Case or box for the *Sefer Torah* used by the Sephardim.

Tishah be'Av
9th of the month of *Av*, a day of fasting in remembrance of the destruction of the First and Second Temples of Jerusalem, 587-86 BCE and 70 CE (see *Av*).

Tishri
1st month of the Jewish calendar, falling around September and October.

Torah
[Precept] 1a. The Pentateuch. 1b. The scroll on which this is written. 2. The whole body of Jewish sacred writings and tradition, including the Mosaic Law (the Pentateuch); the Written Law (the Bible) and the Oral Law (the *Talmud*).

Yad
[Hand] A pointer, in the form of a hand at the end of a long stick, used for reading the *Torah* without touching it.

Yeshivah
A traditional Jewish school.

Zohar
The main text of the cabbala, widely believed to be based on a genuinely ancient original manuscript.

Index of Places